A TRUMPET FOR REASON

by Leo Rosten

A Trumpet for Reason
The Joys of Yiddish
A Most Private Intrigue
The Many Worlds of L*E*O R*O*S*T*E*N
Captain Newman, M.D.
Religions in America [ed.]
The Story Behind the Painting
The Return of H*Y*M*A*N K*A*P*L*A*N
A Guide to the Religions of America
The Dark Corner
112 Gripes About the French [War Department]
Hollywood: The Movie Colony, The Movie Makers
Dateline: Europe
The Strangest Places
The Washington Correspondents
The Education of H*Y*M*A*N K*A*P*L*A*N

A Trumpet for Reason
Leo Rosten

W. H. ALLEN
LONDON AND NEW YORK
1971

© Leo Rosten, 1970
First British edition 1971
Printed in Great Britain by
Fletcher & Son Ltd, Norwich
for the publishers W. H. Allen & Co. Ltd.
Essex Street, London, WC2R 3JG
Bound at Bungay by
Richard Clay (The Chaucer Press) Ltd.

ISBN 0 491 00108 8

For
Joshua, Benjamin, and Pamela

"Students of social science must fear popular approval . . ."

—ALFRED MARSHALL

Contents

PREFACE TO THE ENGLISH EDITION

This book deals, in question and answer form, with that astonishing phenomenon: student rebellion. The scene is the United States, but the analysis and argument are equally germane, I think, to Great Britain. To be sure, America is convulsed by special torments: a ghastly war in Vietnam, the angry upheaval of blacks, an explosively huge (7,000,000!) college population.

Yet without these incendiary elements, campuses as far removed in space and spirit as London, Paris, Berlin, Rome, Tokyo have been made a shambles by youthful passions and revolutionary rages. Even in despotized China, where all-wise Mao officially blessed his new janissary horde of Red Guards, the young zealots turned so fanatic, so messianic, so murderous that the flabbergasted Chairman was driven to the startling extremity of restoring order, if not sanity, to politics by sending college graduates to obscure villages in remote provinces—to live there for life. And in India, students in Satna hacked a proctor to death with knives when he protested the wholesale cheating on examinations; in Gorakhpur, one resourceful stripling brought a fierce Alsatian dog into the classroom and proceeded to answer exam questions by copying them out of the text for the course.

I sometimes wonder how a future Gibbon will explain the rampant irrationality and intolerance of starry-eyed youths who sing of Love but launch "psychodramas masquerading as revolution"? (The phrase is D. L. Gutman's.) And how will a Le Bon unriddle the cult of drugs and dregs and bizarre dress, the ferocious assault on civility, the peculiar "idealism" that mocks reason and turns hooligan? How will a future Macaulay explain the insistence on delinquency as emancipation, the confusion of symbolic patricide with "liberation" politics? How will a Trevor-Roper judge the mindless obscenities of "flower children," the polemical trump-card of plain temper-tantrums, the naïve slogans spun out of ignorance—and utopian delusions? How will a new Lecky explain the singular phenomenon of adult intellectuals who canonize emotionally disturbed adolescents, making them paragons of virtue, successors to the once deified Proletariat?

Some historians, no doubt, will seek parallel phenomena in the Roman Empire after Augustus, or the Dance Craze of the Middle Ages; others will seize upon the fevers and paroxysms of 1848, or the dissolute practices of Berlin in the 1920s. But note this striking preview of today's travail in a different youth movement:

> Turbulent gangs of untidy boys and girls roamed the country. . . . In bombastic words they announced the gospel of a golden age. All preceding generations, they emphasized, were simply idiotic; their incapacity has converted the earth into a hell. But the rising generation is no longer willing to endure gerontocracy, the supremacy of impotent and imbecile senility. Henceforth, brilliant youths will rule. They will destroy everything that is old and useless, they will reject all that was dear to their parents, they will substitute new, real and substantial values . . . for the antiquated and false ones . . .
>
> The inflated verbiage of these adolescents was only a poor disguise for their lack of any ideas and of any definite program. They had nothing to say but this: We are young and therefore chosen; we are ingenious because we are young; we are the carriers of the future; we are the deadly foes of the rotten bourgeois and Philistines. And if somebody was not afraid to ask them what their plans were, they knew only one answer: Our leaders will solve all problems.

The writer of this remarkable passage, Professor von Mises, observes:

It has always been the task of the new generation to provoke changes. But the characteristic feature of the youth movement was that they had neither new ideas nor plans. They called their action the youth movement precisely because they lacked any program (that could) give a name to their endeavors. . . . Their revolutionary radicalism was nothing but the impudence of the years between boyhood and manhood; it was a phenomenon of a protracted puberty. It was void of any ideological content.

And, in a chilling summation:

The chiefs of this youth movement were mentally unbalanced neurotics. Many of them were affected by a morbid sexuality; they were either profligate or homosexual. . . . Their names are long since forgotten; the only trace they left were some books and poems preaching sexual perversity . . .*

To what time and place do these excerpts refer? To Germany —before the First World War.

Metternich once wrote the Austrian minister of education: "I have never feared that the revolution could be produced at the universities; yet I feel certain that a whole generation of revolutionaries is being bred there."

History does repeat itself: not, as Karl Marx quipped, as farce, but in what I, for one, can only mourn as the periodic lunacy of the intelligentsia.

I have tried to provide direct answers to the sweeping charges and flamboyant rhetoric of today's extremists, whether they mouth the foamings of the New Left or the frothings of the Yahoo Right.

I make extensive reference to British scholars, writers and journals; these citations, please notice, were printed long before I dreamed that this testament would be published in London. My mind, which is headquartered in Manhattan, has always been enlarged and enriched from its London office.

LEO ROSTEN

* Ludwig von Mises. *Bureaucracy*, Yale University Press (New Haven), 1944; pp. 94–95.

1. To the Reader

"Fanatics are picturesque; and mankind prefers observing poses to listening to reasons."

—NIETZSCHE

We live in times so violent, so irrational, so ominous, so confused and confusing that this appeal to reason will fall upon many a deaf or derisive ear.

We stand in peril of being stampeded by the oversimplifier, however honest; the fanatic, however idealistic; the unstable, however eloquent; and the naïve, however appealing.

The glittering nostrums of spellbinders have proved so disastrous in this century, and have taken so monstrous a toll in human lives and freedom, that only fools or zealots can rush to repeat both the gullibility and the horrors. Must each generation learn for itself that virtue does not solve equations? That ideology is blind? That when altruists turn militant they become self-righteous tyrants?

Many noble-minded reforms fail because of the subterranean complexity of our problems; others, because of our God-given inability to attain omniscience.

I hasten to add, for the benefit of those who read and run (or riot), that "solutions" to problems much simpler than ours have proven disastrous failures in Socialist heavens—Russia, China, Poland, Cuba, emerging Africa.

We must not mistake noise for weight, anger for argument, good goals for good sense. For passion, like politics, makes very strange bedfellows; it even leads the young to mistake gripes for principles. Hate makes more rebels than Hegel.

I, for one, feel lucky to live in a social order in which I am free to write what I think, criticize whom I please, oppose what I find false or evil. Let the Marcusians sneer that the fact that I think I am free, and even act as if I think I am free, only proves that under the sinister cunning of my oppressors I have been brainwashed to *think* I think I think I am free. Under neo-Marxist microscopes, I am but a deluded pawn of the Establishment, a prisoner of unspeakable repression—a repression triply unspeakable because it operates invisibly and does not use its brutalitarian powers.

The time has arrived for those who believe in freedom to come to the defense of freedom—and reason. Neither can survive if either is destroyed. And both can be destroyed if we allow demagogues, vandals, terrorists, bombers, blackmailers, and romantic bubbleheads with political hallucinations to go unchallenged.

In this time, I find no maxim sounder than Winston Churchill's: "I cannot remain impartial as between the fire brigade and the fire."

In the larger, longer view, my generation has no *right* to bargain away the civil rights we inherited. We have no *right* to bribe bullies, or appease extremists, or surrender to the infantile and the paranoid. We have no right to be cowards.

We have no right to sell or subvert or abandon the citadel of what still is man's last, best hope on earth.

—LEO ROSTEN

May 26, 1970
New York, N.Y.

2. To an Angry Young Man

> "An idealist is one who, upon observing that a rose smells better than a cabbage, concludes that it will also make better soup."
>
> —H. L. MENCKEN

I have read a slew of articles by the young—about their (and our) problems. The writers are bright, articulate, unfailingly earnest. Their grievances, as distinguished from either their knowledge or their reasoning, are often legitimate and moving.

There *is* plenty wrong in this muddled, unjust, fearful world. But our problems are outrageously oversimplified by the innocent and the glib, old *or* young, and by airy assumptions that money, or laws, or Washington, or orators can solve everything. Some human problems simply cannot be solved simply; many simply cannot be solved swiftly; and some cannot be "solved" at all, but can only be ameliorated or reshaped or drained of their poisons.

So much for overture.

This tract began unintentionally, with a rueful paragraph I wrote about the first student riots at Berkeley and Columbia. The response was emphatic: lusty cheers and jeers and a flurry of letters, many long, many detailed, many crammed with astonishing misinformation. The most touching billet-doux ended: "Drop dead!!!" One believer in "honest, open debate" proclaimed me, in the kangaroo court of his rage, a "vicious reactionary imperialist!" The most ecstatic diatribe was signed "Columbia Senior."

I wish I knew to whom and where to send this reply to the overheated:

Dear ?:

It will upset you to learn that I agree with many things you said. For instance:

"Don't question our sincerity!"

I don't. You are about as sincere as anyone can be. You are sincerely unhappy, sincerely frustrated, and sincerely confused. You are also sincerely wrong about the few facts you cite, sincerely befuddled about the inferences to be drawn were the facts true, and sincerely misled by the conclusions you embrace to justify your unreason.

Besides, what on earth does "sincerity" have to do with problems? Any insane asylum hums with sincere patients. Hitler was undoubtedly sincere. So are the followers of Voliva, who sincerely think the world is flat. (The photographs from space, seen through *their* eyes, confirm their conviction, for our earth looks like a crumpled derby with a perfect circle of a rim, a sweet plate—not globe—spinning through God's empyrean.)

I hope you will one day realize that throughout man's history, no group has done more harm, shed more blood, caused more tragedy than those who, sincerely ignorant, added passion to their certitudes. That is what I fear most about sincere you.

> [Youth] have exalted notions, because they have not yet been humbled by life or learnt its necessary limitations. . . . They would always rather do noble deeds than useful ones: their lives are regulated more by moral feeling than by reasoning. . . . All their mistakes are in the direction of doing things excessively and vehemently. . . . They love too much, hate too much; they think they know everything; this, in fact, is why they overdo everything.[1]

Aristotle, whom perhaps you were not required to read, wrote that about 2300 years ago.

"Your generation does not try to communicate with ours."

Is it that I am not "communicating" or that you do not understand what I am saying? It may well be that I am not saying it well. But it may also be that you do not want to hear, or consider, what I say.

It may even be that when communicatees know less than communicators the wail "Failure to communicate!" is both the alibi and the fault of those who complain about it.

"Communication" *does not mean agreeing with you.* I know this will come to you as a shock. But take a moment to calm your indignation: If you don't agree with me, you cry I am wrong. If I don't agree with you, you claim that I don't "under*stand.*" In technical logic, those ploys illustrate the Principle of Unmitigated Gall; in untechnical lingo, they are evidence of unprincipled *chutzpa.*

When the young do try to cope with discombobulating evidence, or fail to find an answer to a pertinent point, they protest: "You are not engaging in a meaningful dialogue!" This graceless cliché is a handy-dandy, all-purpose cop-out, employed whenever an adult has not admitted his supposed sins, or a college knuckled under to preposterous demands.

"Most of our teachers are uninspired, boring, dull. . . ."

I sympathize with you. I, too, nearly suffocated through lectures from withered pedants and conscientious *shlemiels*.

But let's be fair: Is your faculty, by and large, any more uninspired, boring and dull than, say, your classmates? (Don't mistake adolescent agitations for sublime inspiration.) Does not youth always think most adults uninspired and unimaginative? And are there enough competent, intriguing teachers to go around? (Where are they hiding?) And does not your most "uninspired, boring, dull" teacher *know* more about the course he is teaching than you do? I think it fair to say: "Few persons invent algebra on their own."[2]

And have you not yet learned that a silver-tongued charmer is not, beyond the seduction of the moment, necessarily a good teacher? The most popular lecturers are often the best entertainers; the second most loved, of course, are those who flunk no one and praise the prattle of hotheads.

You may learn that you can learn more from a dry scholar than a juicy elocutionist. You can even discipline yourself to trudge up the steep, inevitable hills of education: Dazzling prospects reward some people from the peaks.

Again and again you say:

"The American people want . . . the American people demand . . . Americans insist . . ."

How do you know?

Every poll I have seen until now puts your position in a minority.[3]

You just *say* "the American people demand" or "want" or "insist"—then add whatever you prefer. This is intellectually sloppy, and ethically a sneaky trick.

"The American press and information media do not tell us the truth."

Then how did you learn about all the horrid iniquities you correctly denounce—from Appalachia to black ghettos to the massacre at Song My? (What? . . . Well, where did *he* learn it?)

The American mass media *are* often superficial, inadequate, incomplete, and unclarifying. They cannot help it: They are produced by human beings. But they are also uncensored, and show an independent and refreshing disdain for demagogues, bureaucrats, drum beaters, and even Presidents.

Incidentally, are the mass media as inaccurate or one-sided, as irresponsible or false (that is, undeterred by facts) as, say, the publications of the New Left?

Professor Daniel Bell, a mediating envoy between Columbia's rebels and faculty, has pointed out how easily Mark Rudd and the militants got *their* version of Columbia's alleged "repression" into the newspapers and onto the nation's television networks:

> Emotions were lifted high by songfests and films from Cuba and Vietnam. Red flags were raised from the roofs of two buildings. As national and international attention mounted, famous journalists and poets thrilled to the adventure of being hauled up onto ledges and entering the barricaded buildings through the window, to be told by the embattled students about the inequities of Columbia. (Neither the journalists nor the poets bothered to go to the administration to find out if these stories were true.) . . .
> There was no long history of unresolved conflict. . . . The administration had not been repressive; if anything, it had been, in disciplinary matters, at first lenient and then wayward. . . . History [was] quickly rewritten in order to make it seem that the university was repressive and unresponsive, so as to give a cast of desperation to the action of students, as though no other course was open, or because the issues were so crucial.[4]

A worse fault than you suspect, in the mass media, is their unwitting inflation of young rebels' sense of importance, and—in the undiscriminating drive for more and more news —their overemphasis on the violent, the flamboyant, the shocking, and the aberrant:

> Thus, the typical TV special on the theme, "What Is Happening to Our Youth?", is likely to feature a panel consisting of (1) a ferocious black militant, (2) a feverish member of SDS, (3) a supercilious leader of the Young Americans for Freedom and (4), presumably to represent the remaining 90 per cent, a hopelessly muddled moderate. But we have much the same state of affairs in the quality magazines, where the essays on youth are given to . . . apocalyptic ruminations on the spirit of the young and the imminent decline (or rebirth) of Western civilization.
> Not too surprisingly . . . the most likely writer of these essays is an academic intellectual, teaching humanities or the

social sciences at an elite university. Hence he is exposed, in his office, in his classes, to far more than the usual number of radical or hippie-esque students.[5]

"We will destroy a system that has not abolished war, unemployment, exploitation!"

By the same reasoning, let's execute all doctors, destroy all biologists, decapitate all researchers, and blow up all hospitals: After all, they have not abolished disease.

Before you destroy this system, which has evolved through so much pain and experiment and human agony, why not propose another that *will* solve (not hide, shift, or disguise) the problems of unemployment and exploitation and war.

Unemployment, for instance: There is no unemployment in a prison. Or a concentration camp. Or where officials can transform strikers into slaves.

War? Did not wars rage during all the centuries before "this system" existed? What plagues the human race is that it takes two (or three or four) to keep the peace, but only one to start the shooting. I hate war as war can be hated only by those who lived through two worldwide wars and their horrendous aftermaths. Yet the ancient, sobering truth prevails: "If you want peace, be prepared for war."

If you will stage your peace demonstrations in Washington *and* Hanoi *and* Peking *and* Moscow *and* Cairo *and* Tel Aviv *and* . . . I, and a legion of the unbellicose, will gladly join you.

Any simpleton can proclaim the millennium—no war, no cruelty, no hunger, no greed—just as any demagogue can promise Utopia, without revealing a shred of competence or a program. When asked what the New Left proposed to do if it achieved power, Tom Hayden, an early messiah, replied: "First we'll make the revolution—then we'll find out what for."

Heavens to Betsy! Would you hire a plumber who wants to rip out all the pipes in town before he figures out how to repair a leak in your sink? . . . Yes, I'm afraid you would: That's what little rebels are made of: touching compassion, a dream of creating heaven on earth—fast, and the most astonishing ignorance about such trivia as how milk is delivered, or how jobs are made, or how to raise the standard of living, or what functions a bank serves, or how to allocate resources, or what kind of incentives can replace personal gain without crippling personal freedom, or how to choose between critical priorities, or what urban problems entail, or why slum clearance fails, or why "soaking the rich" injures the poor, or when raising taxes proves counterproductive, or when our foreign aid harms an underdeveloped country, etc., etc., etc.

A little knowledge is dangerous—unless it creates respect for the dimensions of problems and their intricate, interlocked conjunction with others.

A total lack of knowledge deserves no respect.

And ignorance parading as truth, with sanguine auguries of universal salvation, is nothing less than deception.

"This rotten system is run by nincompoops who are nothing but politicians."

Venice depends on "nothing but" gondoliers.

The politician serves an essential function in a free land. He mediates between inevitable conflicts of interests.

The alternative to the politician is what? A dictator and his sycophants? Bureaucrats protected from public opinion because they need not stand for election? Official parrots of a party line? Intellectuals? (Caution: No one is more dangerous, given too much power; superior minds tend to resent, and are alienated from, the masses.*)

Politics is not a demon spawned by this system. Politics is a process, inevitable in all human groupings—even those governed by sanctified ritual or a hereditary hierarchy. Politics thrives in a labor union, a garden club, the SDS, the Museum of Modern Art, the Black Muslims. (Who killed Malcolm X?)

In some lands, the political stakes are life itself. Here, those who lose at the polls are not beaten or jailed or murdered, but are free to seek power again.

Every human group seeks power or influence, at the final (if unforeseen or remote) expense of others.

As for the breezy crack that our politicians are "nincompoops," I will cheerfully match the intelligence, to say nothing of the common sense, of the American Senate against that of any college faculty you choose.

I read with sadness your familiar incantation:

"We want a society in which humane leaders have the power to abolish all injustice. . . ."

The "humane leaders" who exercise the power to abolish injustice consistently become egomaniacal, arbitrary, stupid,

---

* Consider the crucial role played in Washington, vis-à-vis Vietnam, for instance, by bona fide intellectuals: Dean Rusk, McGeorge Bundy, Walt Rostow, Henry Kissinger—not one of whom can be called a "war profiteer" or a militarist.

jealous, ruthless, odious, erratic, hypocritical, self-intoxi-
cated, self-aggrandizing, capricious, blind, irresponsible,
treacherous, shameless, savage, barbarous, criminal, merci-
less, murderous, and insane. Please note:

Every adjective after the word "become" is taken from
official statements and speeches by Marxist leaders, about
their once revered colleagues, at home or abroad. Outraged
readers should address their chastisements to Peking,
Havana, Prague, Moscow, Warsaw, Budapest, Bucharest,
the capital of purified Romania, and Tirana, the capital of
enlightened Albania.

> The idealists who make a revolution are bound to be disap-
> pointed. . . . For at best their victory never dawns on the
> shining new world they had dreamed of, cleansed of all human
> meanness. Instead it dawns on a familiar, workaday place, still
> in need of groceries and sewage disposal. The revolutionary
> state, under whatever political label, has to be run not by
> violent romantics but by experts in marketing, sanitary engineer-
> ing, and the management of bureaucracies. For the Byrons
> among us, this discovery is a fate worse than death.[6]

"Our college courses are outrageously irrelevant."

I sadly agree; for your letters reveal that you could not
pass an elementary exam in at least three fields in which
you pass such sweeping judgments: economics, history,
political theory. I say nothing about your ignorance of tests
for the validation of data, or the processes of inference and
proof.

"Irrelevant?" To what? For whom? By which criteria?
At which stage of which undertaking?

Our college courses may be inadequate (which is different

from irrelevant), but they do present the most we *know* about social problems so vast that the increases in our knowledge often extend the boundaries of our ignorance and unhappily complicate what we are studying. Don't blame the swimmer for the tides, or the scientist for the perversities of the atom.

Euclid may not be "relevant" to a man who wants to be a halfback, tree surgeon, or grommet puncher. But can anyone deny the debt mankind owes to, say, Euclid's "irrelevances"? Most of you are alive only because of men who pursued "irrelevant" ideas. A lens grinder, refining his magnifiers until he began to see "little beasties," unknowingly founded bacteriology. Einstein was surely as irrelevant as anyone can be. Computers, like penicillin, began in irrelevant wonder. So did guitars, airplanes, and marijuana.

I think college itself is irrelevant—for a great many of you, who should not be there at all. College is certain to frustrate those who seek panaceas, who don't want knowledge for its own sake and beauty and self-enrichment, who don't enjoy learning how to use the instrumentalities of the mind, who are bored by long, vexatious study, who cannot endure the prolongation of analysis, the sustaining of abstraction, the random and exciting excursions of curiosity. (The one thing curiosity cannot be is "idle.")

You seem to think that whatever does not give you instant, absolute answers to vast and amorphous questions is irrelevant. But significance is more important than relevance. Kingman Brewster, President of Yale, not unloved by the young, recently wrote:

> "Relevance" may not be best. . . . Impetuous action, conscious oversimplification, refusal to doubt, and the rejection of reason are enemies of the university. . . .[7]

May I suggest a solution to those who are unbearably unhappy with the irrelevant? Quit college. Work—in whatever field or group you find relevant to your yearnings. You may learn from experience, then return to college with more mature expectations. If you want to immerse yourself in a totally relevant, useful, self-freeing endeavor, drive a cab. In New York.*

In 1965 Professor Joseph Tussman, University of California philosopher, enthusiastically started a new "humanized" school on the edge of the campus for 150 freshmen, who would spend two years liberated from conventional, "irrelevant" college courses. The 150 students hugely enjoyed themselves, it appeared, especially during final exams. But in 1970 Professor Tussman bitterly said:

> The educational system is a farce, but to let students tell you how to remake it is equivalent to letting the sickest patients take over the practice of medicine because doctors often make mistakes.
>
> People who call themselves radicals have adopted the slogan that "the customer is always right"—in a strange kind of long-hair capitalism. The result is turmoil.[8]

Another professor at Berkeley's brave new Center for Participant Education remarked on how the curriculum swiftly sank into courses on mysticism and astrology, "Getting in Touch" and "Loving Responsibility," and dourly concluded: "We have learned that the students have no ideas. They come up with nutty things like Marxism taught by a Zen Buddhist."[9]

The most striking comment I have encountered on relevance in college courses comes from Professor Robert Nis-

---

* One veteran cabby told me: "I work when I want and drive where I want, and if I'm sleepy I just turn over in bed, and if it's snowing I don't go out at all but stay home and watch a ball game. I eat when I want and I stop work for as long as I want for a coke or a cuppa coffee. Mister, I've got no *boss!* I'm a free man. . . . I'd go nuts working indoors."

bet, who has spent thirty-five years at the University of California:

> The curriculum, it was said, must be made relevant to the interests and needs of students. I would not wish to even guess at the vast number of newspaper editorials and television commentaries that solemnly and dutifully echoed this cry. It was appealing.
>
> It was also appalling. For invariably what the student cry for relevance turned out to be was the all-too-familiar middle-class child's cry to be entertained, to be stimulated, above all, to be *listened to*, no matter what or how complex the subject at hand. Having become accustomed in their homes to get attention to whatever was on their minds, and of course incessant and lavish praise for their "brightness," is it not to be expected that when the children go off to the university the same attention should be given their interests and needs?
>
> Revamping curricula and colleges into student-planned "sensitivity," "great books," and "encounter" groups is little more, I should think, than a kind of final solution for this middle-class sprung ache to be recognized—constantly and everlastingly.[10]

Insofar as the *substance* of a subject or course goes, the cry for relevance usually turns out to be a demand for some special viewpoint or preferential bias:

> One of our most solemn obligations is to state truth as we see it and to refuse to allow any of our courses to become instruments of propaganda. The world has seen the dreadful consequences of Aryan History instead of history, and of Communist Genetics instead of genetics. Courses whose primary purposes are political or racial indoctrination have no place in our educational system—no matter who demands them or what noble purposes they may seem to serve.[11]

It is precisely the faddist subjects, the visionary gropings toward self-fulfillment, the maudlin "encounters," the discredited occult "sciences" that attract the alienated or those who hate the discipline of getting educated.

The results can be predicted, I think: The products of "liberated" curriculums will be bitterly disappointed, unless they retreat into a permanent break with reality, in new flights of fantasy or the prison of autism. The rest will return, to either college or life, chastened, confused, more ravenous than ever for enlightenment (psychological, if not substantive), still yearning for some quick, magical truth that may reduce the ravages of their discontent—with themselves.

"This society is only interested in higher prices and profits! We want a system of production for use."

You apparently do not understand this society, or *a* society, or the function of prices (and profits) in *any* economy.

Has it never occurred to you that the market place is a polling booth? That buying is voting? That no economic system operates without *some* form of pricing, without some yardstick for allocating resources, without some measure of efficacy and worth? Has it never occurred to you that profits are a form of proof—that a product or a service satisfies those who freely pay for it? Have you examined the public uses we make of private profits—through taxation?

Consider the countries that follow your platitude, "production for use." *Without a single exception,* they produce far less for their people to enjoy, of much shoddier quality, at much higher prices (measured by the hours of work needed to buy something).[12]

Don't you know that socialist countries are everywhere smuggling capitalist incentives into their systems? Not just base Brezhnev, but noble Castro (who for ten years attacked those who doubted his reckless claims about the sugar harvest) and mighty Mao have lately stunned their followers by publicly announcing egregious failures in performance, fatal flaws in their plans, bafflingly inadequate "incentives" to their masses.[13] The Russians, after fifty-three years(!) of total power, must ask Henry Ford and Italian automakers to come to the proletarian paradise—to make cars.

Has it not dawned on you that wherever and whenever there is no free market, there is no free thought, no free art, no free politics, no free life?

Can you name one country where individual freedom does not rest on private property and a middle class?

"The middle class exploits the unemployed."

Please examine that cliché.

Would the middle class be worse off or better off if you could wave a magic wand and make all the unemployed disappear? Obviously, the middle class would be much better off: Think of the enormous saving in taxes, the improvement in public services, the benefits from refocused energies now used to ameliorate poverty's abominable toll.

And as a minor benefit, consider the psychological relief of not having to contend, again and again, with the same old Marxist misconceptions.

"We will build a dozen Peace Corps [and] repair the insidious work of Wall Street."

The Peace Corps was an admirable, altruistic conception, administered by some of the most attractive people I knew in the Kennedy administration. The Corps was joined by scores of excellent, able, compassionate people. That the impetus and fervor of the Peace Corps have flagged is not without meaning. Here is one ironic explanation:

> Presumably, a Peace Corps volunteer who teaches an illiterate Brazilian to read, without hope of profit, is doing more for the illiterate Brazilian than General Electric does for Brazil when it hires teachers to teach the illiterate members of its work force to read, in the hope that it can reduce its supervisory costs and increase its profits.
>
> The end result is the same. Illiterate Brazilians learn to read.
>
> But the motive is different. Somehow that means that the Peace Corps volunteer has contributed to the "welfare" of poor Brazilians and G.E. has not. The Peace Corps volunteer was not motivated by self-interest [except to the extent that he desires travel, adventure, and instant status—at minimum cost] while G.E. was motivated by a lust for profit.[14]

Reality is full of such paradoxes, which are lost upon idealists who see in the dreadful poverty of a Central American jungle, or the appalling malnutrition of an African village, the nefarious, conspiratorial, omnipotent hand of "Wall Street."

How the foreign poor would profit if Wall Street would only channel investment funds into productive enterprises, and supply jobs, wages, food, education, medicine—all the things our bravoes of the New Left take for granted, whose origins and underpinnings they know not of.

"We want a really free society in which the radical young can speak their minds against the Establishment."

Where in the name of heaven do the young speak and publish and protest more freely, recklessly, and intransigently? Where on earth do the young more openly attack the Establishment? (Every political order has one.)

Wherever *your* heroes—Marx, Mao, Ché—have prevailed, students, writers, teachers, scientists have been punished with hard labor or death. For what? For their opinions. For their poems. For their stories. For insufficient subservience to monolithic dogma. Certainly not for demonstrating —which is forbidden or repressed with ferocity.

I cannot help thinking of one professor's questions:

> Why, one wonders, are practically all campus newspapers in the hands of the extreme left? Why are the student unions and student funds controlled by militant minorities? Why don't the administration and the faculty demand a student referendum on these matters—with compulsory voting if that is needed to make student elections meaningful?
>
> The reason, I suspect, is that they fear the left would lose —and would then be even more troublesome than it is. So, fearful of democracy they try bribery, with predictable results.[15]

Where *except* in this "fake democracy" you despise are mass demonstrations possible? And protected? And where else is bitter and legitimate dissent so widely and openly reported, radioed, televised, discussed? Where has youth more persistently registered its discontents? Where have so many tried so hard to understand youth's grievances?

You protest that you have not been effective? But you have—very effective (see Chapter 3). Your real complaint, the fury and frustration that fuel your activity, rests on the fact that you have not prevailed. You do not want discussion; you want surrender. You do not seek "liberation"; you want power.

"America's leaders are corrupted and crazed with power. They deceive the people."

Your leaders demand that power, which would equally craze them. They deceive you in not telling you how they plan confrontations deliberately designed to force the police to use force, whose excesses I hate more than you do. I, unlike you, want no one put "up against the wall."

No "cheap politician" ever more cynically deceived you than your inflammatory orators have done—and will do. Your fervent, credulous support feeds their neurotic (because extremist) needs. Washington's "Nonviolent" Coordinating Committee (SNCC) used gunfire for three days, September 6–9, 1968, to prove their love of non-violence. As for the Maoists and Weathermen: Who disputes their naked and violent bid for power?

Item, not wholly irrelevant: Fidel Castro, in his first appearance before the cheering multitudes in Havana, used this not admirable gimmick to enhance his charisma: White doves fluttered around his head and perched on his shoulders and whispered supernal messages into his ear—where he had providentially placed corn or seeds.[16]

"How can you defend a system where there is so much misery?"

Because the system does not create only (and all) the misery, and because I can't find El Dorado: Witness the suicide, alcoholism, crime, divorce, and delinquency rates in other systems or countries.

I, too, once asked your very question, and believed in its verity and implications. The works of the Webbs and the Hammonds, depicting the inhuman effects of the Industrial Revolution and capitalism, were gospel to my generation of radicals/liberals.

Research has blown most of the air out of the myth. The fact is that after endless centuries of excruciating poverty and misery and hopelessness, it was the factory system that saved the poor, gave them jobs and tools, produced better food and clothes and shelter, presented unprecedented opportunities to the millions.

Those who moved into the stinking slums of English cities from the lovely England countryside moved out of stinking barns and hovels and ditches. They went to the machines to get a precious job, to live better and aspire higher.[17] The same is true of the millions of immigrants who flocked to American sweatshops—from the hunger and hopelessness of Ireland, Italy, eastern Europe.

Capitalism replaced not Arcadia, but indescribable poverty, illiteracy, and economic doom.

It was under "heartless capitalism," believe it or not, that the earnings of the masses soared; and as men became *less* poor their discontents grew louder and their social protest and political power boomed into a force such as had not existed within any political system before.

"We will build a world based on idealism—whatever the costs!"

It takes no brain to be idealistic. It also costs nothing—at first. And idealism can be dragged out to justify *any* acts that self-proclaimed idealists choose to commit, any laws they choose to break, any liberties they choose to supersede.

I went to Russia, had long talks with Lenin and other prominent men, and saw as much as I could of what was going on. I came to the conclusion that everything that was being done and . . . intended was totally contrary to what any person of a liberal outlook would desire. I thought the regime already hateful and certain to become more so. I found the source of evil in a contempt for liberty and democracy which was a natural outcome of fanaticism.

It was thought by radicals in those days that one ought to support the Russian Revolution, whatever it might be doing, since it was opposed by reactionaries, and criticism of it played into their hands. I . . . was for some time in doubt as to what I ought to do. But in the end I decided in favor of what seemed to me to be the truth. I stated publicly that I thought the Bolshevik regime abominable, and I have never seen any reason to change this opinion.

[Russia] seemed to me one vast prison in which the jailers were cruel bigots. When I found my friends applauding these men as liberators and regarding the regime they were creating as a paradise, I wondered . . . whether it was my friends or I who were mad. . . .[18]

Before you dismiss this as the propaganda of an agent of capitalist imperialism, you should know who wrote it: the man who later became the world's foremost opponent of American intervention in Vietnam, a lifelong pacifist, the idol and defender of youth throughout the world, one of the commanding minds of our century: Bertrand Russell.

As for your final note of bravado, "whatever the costs," that means cost to *others;* and that is how romantic idealists become dictators, or justify the savageries of a Robespierre or a Lenin or a Hitler. Idealism has no right to be despotic.

Youth is impatient; its leaders, intractable. Do they have the faintest notion of the terrible punishment *any* revolution imposes—even on the faithful? While the faithful dream of the brotherhood of man, their idols institute the grim, deadly processes by which they can get what *they* want. This is done through killings, torture, propaganda and terror.

No one can foresee where violence will end. The Robespierres and Madame Rolands die on the guillotine; the Slanskys perish in dungeons; the Trotskys end in exile/murder. Revolutions *do* devour their own.

"We will wipe the blight of racism and prejudice from the earth."

I wish you could. I wish you would. And I wish you would start within your own ranks.

Michael Lerner, who is under thirty and edited the Harvard *Crimson,* wrote a brilliant article in the *American Scholar* called "Respectable Bigotry," and reports the "hidden, liberal-radical bigotry" he found in the SDS and among middle-class militants.[19]

Racism is not confined to whites. Ask any Puerto Rican or African or Arab, any Chinese or untouchable or Caribbean East Indian. In some colleges (Northwestern, Cornell), anti-racist white students were, to their embarrassment, driven to support segregation—a segregation deliberately sought and established by black students in all-black dormitories. (The fact that this violated state laws against segregation did not deter those who live in Topsy-Turvy land.)

The Guardian, a New Left journal, no hireling of the Establishment, published this memorable report of the 1969 SDS National Convention:

> Chaka Walls, minister of information of the Illinois Black Panther Party . . . explain[ed] the role of women in the revolution. "We believe in the freedom of love, in pussy power," he said. A shock wave stunned the arena, and PL [Progressive Labor] responded with chants of "Fight male Chauvinism."
>
> Anger was so intense that Walls stepped down and left the podium to Jewel Cook, another Panther spokesman. Cook, not understanding what was wrong with "pussy power" . . . said: "Walls was only trying to say that you sisters have a strategic position for the revolution . . . prone."[20]

Suppose a white, anti-feminist, Southern red-neck oaf had said that?

You must surely know that the most vicious treatment accorded blacks in our hemisphere is found not in Mississippi or Watts, but in the horrible republic of Haiti. You must surely suspect, by now, that xenophobia is endemic to man, and is not the accursed syndrome limited to whites —who despise, snub, hate, and fight each other, too.

You should know that prejudice exists *without* those characteristics you mistake for cause: color, economic exploitation, job competition, residential proximity, urban pressures.[21] The persecution and slaughter of Jews by Christians had nothing to do with race (the Jews are Caucasians) or color. The savagery inflicted on Armenians and Greeks was nationalist and religious in origin. And you might pause to consider how many decent, law-abiding Americans disapproved of the Pirenians, the Wallonians and the Danerians. The fact that these minorities were invented by the researching pollster did not diminish the hostility against anything different.[22]

There has arisen a new, guilt-expiating prejudice, which takes the form of automatically transferring all virtue to a group—any group—that has been subjected to prejudice. I see no more reason to say that everything black students want should be given them than to say that everything black students want should be denied them. (I even dislike the label "black students," since many black students are the reluctant pawns of their leaders.) I see no more sense in justifying violence by blacks than in rationalizing violence by whites.

Prejudice is prejudice, whatever its disguises. Prejudice suspends judgment, ignores evidence, and refuses to reason. The recent suburbanite glorification of those blacks who preach terror would be outrageous if the apprentice criminals were white; why—except in the peculiar irrationality of *mea culpa* flagellants—should criminality be excused, much less financed, on the *reversed* predilections of race?

It is disheartening to have to repeat the obvious. Prejudice festers in many forms besides color: in religion, tribalism, caste, nationalism, politics itself.[23] Only the purblind ignore the murderous furies of blacks against blacks in the Congo, the horrors inflicted by Nigeria on the Ibo, the anti-Chinese mania unleashed in the genocide in Indonesia, the slaughter by the Viet Cong—at Hue, in Cambodia and Laos—of fellow Vietnamese.

Finally, as to prejudice: Who is more dogmatic, more intolerant, more prejudging than the New Left? Some of your leaders even defend the nauseating anti-Semitism of Moscow and Warsaw.

"The brutality of the police forces us to take counter-action, to throw rocks, break windows, smash the pigs. . . ."

At Berkeley, at Columbia, at San Francisco State, at Cornell, at Harvard, at Santa Barbara, etc., etc. the breaking of laws, the disruption of the peace, the eruption of vandalism, the capture of buildings, the setting of fires, the use of bombs, the chaining of doors, the rifling of files, the employing of bullhorns to drown out dissent—all these preceded the appearance of the police, who were called only after campus demagogues stymied college presidents and demoralized ambivalent faculties.

> Radicals of the left historically have used those tactics to incite the extreme right with the calculated design of fostering a regime of repression from which the radicals of the left hope to emerge as the ultimate victor. The left in that role is the provocateur. . . . The social compact has room for tolerance, patience, and restraint, but not for sabotage and violence.[24]

In case you are wondering who wrote this, it was Supreme Court Justice William O. Douglas.

At Columbia, a participant in the events reported: "The SDS leadership certainly wanted the police to come. As one of them said later, 'The eyes of Berlin were upon us and we wanted the police to come in and drag us out.' They did."[25]

Those who doubt the calculated tactic of provoking police

action might profit from the analysis made by Howard Hubbard, "Five Long Hot Summers and How They Grew."[26] This study traces the strategy employed by student generals to force brutal police responses to student activism. The "repressive" response guarantees a moral victory, and a propaganda weapon of priceless value.

From Berkeley to Wisconsin to Columbia to Harvard, all the evidence reinforces the old maxim of European revolutionists: No demonstration should be considered successful unless it provokes the authorities to use the police against the demonstrators. The more police violence, the easier the charges of brutality—and the better for the cause.

The young unwisely fail to realize that the "pigs" will have to protect the extremist Left from the extremist Right. The Left is quite incapable of conducting a successful revolution (Labor and farmers—we lack peasants—loathe our "overprivileged youth"), but the Left *can* precipitate a vicious counterreaction—as happened in New York in May 1970. The "hard hat" construction workers who inflicted their indefensible violence on pacific wearers of beards and blue jeans were finally deterred—by whom? The police. And the Left complained that the police were not enforcing law and order! I could only sigh for the summer patriot. I commend to you these lines from Shakespeare:

> We must not make a scarecrow of the law,
> Setting it up to fear the birds of prey,
> And let it keep one shape, till custom make it
> Their perch and not their terror.[27]

In one phrasing or another you say:

"This is a heartless country in which the poor get poorer. . . ."

Alas, poor Yoricks: The *decline* in poverty in the United States is among the more astonishing and hopeful facts of human history:

In 1900 about 90 per cent of our population was poor; in 1920—50 per cent; in 1930—34 per cent; in 1960—22 per cent; in 1969—13 per cent.[28] (Yes, the poverty line, as defined by the Social Security Administration, does take rising prices into account.)

You will reply that 13 per cent is outrageous. I agree. The question is: How best abolish it? A negative income tax makes more sense than anything your colleagues propose. The Council of Economic Advisers reported in 1969 that poverty can be entirely eliminated in ten years.[29]

As for the causes and sources of poverty, a case can be made for the fact that a sizable portion of our problem is the unhappy consequence of long-standing, well-meaning, but economically counterproductive *government* programs that introduced rigidities, contradictions, and waste— of money, brains, skill, time, resources—into the complex enough economic equilibrium.[30]

Does this outrage you? It should.

Does this surprise you? It wouldn't, if you had done some homework.

London's *Economist* recently observed:

America draws its poverty line at levels that would be considered generous abroad. Amid all the sad statistics poured forth about the ghettos, it is worth remembering that in 1967 some 88 percent of all black American families had a television set.[31]

A common protest, so widely uttered, is your plaintive:

"Our generation wants to be understood."

So does mine. How much have you tried to understand us?

You pillory us for injustices not of our making, conflicts not of our choice, dilemmas that history (or our forebears or the sheer intractability of events) handed us.

You say we have "failed" you. I say that you are failing *us*—in failing to learn and respect some discomforting facts; in using violence to shut down colleges; in shamefully denying freedom to others to speak, study, and teach; in vilifying those who disagree with you; in failing to see how much more complicated social problems are than you blindly assume; in acting out of an ignorance for which idealism is no excuse, and a hysteria for which youth is no defense.

"Understanding"? You don't even understand that when you call me a "mother f——" you are projecting your unresolved incestuous wishes onto me. The technical name for such projection, in advanced form, is paranoia.

"We will wreck this unjust, slow, inefficient 'democratic' state."

It took the human race centuries of thought and pain, suffering and experiment, to devise it.

Democracy is not a "state" but a process. It is a way of solving human problems, a way of hobbling power, a way of protecting every minority from the awful, fatal tyranny of either the few or the many.

Whatever its imperfections, which are open and responsive to political contest, democracy is the only system the race of man has so far invented that makes possible *change without violence*. Beware those who disparage the magnitude of this. The slow process of legislation is surely better than that power Chairman Mao described as coming "from the barrel of a gun"—or the thongs of a whip, or the long, silent murder of imprisonment and exile.

Do you really prefer bloodshed to debate? Führers to laws? Guns to elections? Bombs to due process?

This democracy you deride made possible a great revolution in the past thirty-five years in these United States: a profound rearrangement of power, a remarkable redistribution of wealth, unprecedented improvements in living and health—without "liquidating" millions, without suppressing free speech, without the obscenities of dogmas enforced by terror.

This "slow, inefficient" system protects people like me against people like you; and (though you don't realize it) protects innocents like you against those "reactionary . . . fascist forces" you fear: They, like you, "prefer action to talk."

As for the security you apostrophize: At what price? The most secure of human institutions is a prison; would you choose to live in one?

Rallies and bravado and riots are delicious escapes from boredom. They serve as instant therapy to the bored. (In Berkeley and Harvard, during the peaks of student activism, there was a dramatic drop in the number of students coming to the college health services for psychiatric help.[32])

But your pipe dreams about "wrecking," "uprooting," and

"destroying" America overnight make me sigh—not in despair, but in pity for such naïveté: Rome was not burned in a day.

"Herbert Marcuse shows that 'democratic' capitalist freedom actually enslaves."

Professor Marcuse doesn't "show"—he only *says*.

He certainly does not sound enslaved.

And does mouthing fragments of nineteenth-century ideologues such as Marx, Hegel, Sorel, Bakunin really liberate? And is not Marcuse forty years "older than thirty," your cutoff point for trust? (Incidentally, would you entrust your life to a brain surgeon under thirty who never finished medical school?)

If I understand Professor Marcuse correctly (and there is every chance I do) he maintains that we believe we are free because we have been hornswoggled into thinking so. What true freedom would be, à la Marcuse, is a dictatorship of the (his) dogmatic. He has confessed that a "certain amount" of censorship will be needed to prevent "certain" teachers from "corrupting" students; and he even has—but you will hear more about Dr. Marcuse later.

The fundamental trouble with the anarchist is that, though he may be highly intelligent, he has no sense. A fruitful discussion of anarchism is almost an impossibility. If they do not realize that they have set their net among the stars, no word of man will persuade them that their thoughts are moving in a world unreal and unrealizable.

Anarchists are a race of highly intelligent and imaginative children.[33]

I close this painful letter by saying that your irrationality makes me wonder how you were ever admitted *into* college.

You confuse rhetoric with reasoning. Assertions are not facts. Passion is no substitute for knowledge. Slogans are not solutions.

And when you dismiss our differences with contempt, you become contemptible.

Very *sincerely* yours,

LEO ROSTEN

P.S. Please don't take any more courses in sociology. It seduces the immature into thinking they understand a problem if they discuss it in polysyllables.

Jargon is not insight.

Vocabulary is the opiate of our radicals.

3. To an Angry Old Man

> "It is the mistake of youth to think
> imagination a substitute for experience;
> it is the mistake of age to think experi-
> ence a substitute for intelligence."
> —LYMAN BRYSON
> (paraphrased)

I could massage your heartstrings or curl your hair, depending on your politics, by quoting from the torrential reaction to my evangelical letter *To an Angry Young Man*. Before it was printed, a friend urged me to soften my words, saying, "It may play into the hands of the Right." Of the sentiments you are about to read, others will undoubtedly say, "They will play into the hands of the Left."

Both positions seem to me indefensible. Surely, the validity of an idea has nothing to do with who agrees or disagrees with it. To censor your thinking because of whom it may please or displease is to let others do your thinking for you. I oppose thought control.

Here, without apology, is my answer to some agitated correspondents from the Right.

Dear Messrs. Gruntled and Disgruntled:

Thank you for writing—and that's about all the thanks you'll get from me.

You say,

"Let's throw all these young rebels out of college!"

Over my dead body.

Free speech does not stop at the gates of a campus. On the contrary, it should find special encouragement and protection there. It is the heart, brain, and soul of the search for truth.

A student has a perfect right to argue, disagree, question. He has a perfect right to dissent, denounce, picket, and petition. He has the same right to exercise his constitutional rights as you do.

What he does not have a right to do is turn dissent into terrorism or vandalism or mayhem. He has no right to break the law—even under the self-declared special privilege of academic "immunity." The simple fact is that when students use force, take hostages, set fires, throw rocks, stop others from attending classes, and riot, they stop acting as students and become lawbreakers. The law must attend to them—the swifter the better.

But *you* want students thrown out of school simply for expressing their opinions. Has it not occurred to you that that is exactly what the Communists and Fascists do, from Russia to Spain, China to Cuba? *They* intimidate, expel, and imprison those who question or comment or complain.

To defend democracy by dictatorial methods is to subvert and betray it. Patriotism is not served by vigilantes. What on earth do you think police are *for?*

I oppose your position as much as I oppose the New Left's, and as you both no doubt loathe mine. You and they have more in common with each other than either of you has in common with me. You have no more right to throw them off campus for their beliefs than they have to intimidate your sons and daughters for theirs.

"Draft these college punks into the Army and let our GIs knock sense into their heads!"

You horrify me. I don't want anyone to "knock sense" into anyone's head. Sense is not a function of muscle, or misguided "Americanism." The militant Left spreads its version of sense through hit-and-run raids, Molotov cocktails, and the riot tactics of experienced *provocateurs*. Will you really emulate them?

To put the point more sharply, let me quote a folk jurist: "Your freedom to move your fist ends at the point where my nose begins." I have a long nose.

As for the draft: Before the report of the President's Commission on an All-Volunteer Armed Force,[34] I wrote that I thought the draft impractical, unnecessary, and morally indefensible. It penalizes the sons of the poor, the poor student, and the non-college male. It creates an army of reluctant soldiers whose training period, or combat experience, trods hard on the heels of the end of their service—which requires the costly training of new draftees and the continuing inefficiencies of a continually replaced body of inexperience. The draft uses slave labor, in effect, paying men ("our boys") wages far below what they deserve and can get. It takes several years of income earning and experience out of a young man's life—without compensation. Above all, it ignores the fact that in any large population, a considerable number of young men are attracted to army life, *esprit*, travel, and even combat. There are surely more soldiers, by temperament, than percussionists or tightrope walkers. There will be far more enlistees if we pay more to attract them, and do not penalize—through low wages or high scorn— those who enjoy the military life and believe in its honor and status.

The young have every right to speak, petition, and argue against the draft (this has nothing to do with Vietnam). They have no right to become a mob, to burn a Selective Service office, to harass ROTC "jocks," or refuse to allow others to follow *their* political predilections. (Why, incidentally, the Left attacks campus ROTC as a voluntary activity can be explained only in terms of its propaganda value—plus an unwise acceptance of a diabolized stereotype. Surely it is better for future soldiers to get a humanistic education, and maintain contact with unmilitary students and teachers. To force the military into segregated communities is foolish—and dangerous.)

"Why let these creeps wear stinking clothes, filthy beards, and weird hairdos? Line them up, hold them down, bathe them, shave them, wash out their mouths with soap!!"

I loathe your bully-boy views more than their flamboyant costumes or their childish regression to defiant untidiness.

Kooky clothes and freaky hairdos break no laws (though courts *have* ruled on the right of school boards to govern dress, hair, etc.). Young slobs may pollute the nearby air, but the courts have not yet ruled on how close they may come to you, or vice versa.

They love beads and safari hats, Confederate coats and military costumes from God knows what army or junk shop —I find them colorful, amusing, sometimes saddening, but surely not sinful. They are stabs at self-expression, youth's perennial drive to look unique, to look interesting, to set itself off from all others.

In my college days, we ironed the front brim of our hats upward, put metal click-plates on our heels (to stamp our virility into older ears), and wore yellow raincoats on which we painted dashing half-witticisms. We also danced the Black Bottom, the Dip, and those frenetic oscillations called the Charleston. I cannot see that anyone was damaged, physically or spiritually, by this adolescent *lèse-majesté* against the staid mores. It helped relieve the frustrations, the interminable waiting, the stormy moods of teen-agery.

When today's young break out of the cocoon of safe, respectable, permissive families, they need compensatory sustenance. Teachers "put them down," refute their assertions, question their evidence, strip their defenses, puncture their posings. Teachers *grade* them, and even write "Failed." No, no: Teachers are cardboard parents. It is their own age group from whom the unanchored get reinforcement—mirrors that show what one wants to see.

So the young move in conforming packs, proclaiming their non-conformity. They dress alike, act alike, talk alike—paradoxically insisting on the right to "do their own thing." The lofty enemies of materialism are surprisingly materialistic, spending their parents' money quite generously on hi-fi sets, cars, travel, $3 admission-per-head movies, and LP collections. The aesthetes who so despise "gross bourgeois values" are surprisingly self-indulgent and sensual: acolytes of orgiastic music, primitive rhythms, and—drugs. Historians will surely note that the sons and daughters of an affluent middle class flaunted the fake work shirts and Levis of proletarians, cowboys, floaters, derelicts.

Young men whose hair resembles decaying chrysanthemums still startle me. Girls whose carefully frayed, skin-tight slacks are artfully spattered with paint, to suggest the Dionysian artist, delight me. The wilder, slovenly garb, aping the dishevelment of hermits and crackpots, makes me sad; it reminds me of the disorder of a mental ward.

But you, sir, can relax: Fashion runs in cycles, and shuttles between extremes: mini-skirts will give way to long coats; short, trim haircuts were superseded by Bohemian long hair—which will be replaced by another idiosyncrasy designed to magnify "individuality"—that is, departure from whatever adults favor.

During the French Revolution, the libertarian females bared their breasts to symbolize their final and triumphant liberation from sex discrimination. Today's brave, far-out young iconoclasts wear what? The long hair of Victorian times; the gewgaws, lockets, sashes that long lay in grandmothers' attics. The male bravoes have retrogressed, in their progress, to the pendants, baubles, fancy belts, and ruffles of eighteenth-century dandies. I would not be surprised if some daring young rebel started a craze for snuffboxes, monocles, and dickeys. (Eyeglasses already have reverted to the round, metal-rimmed variety used by antebellum spinsters and storekeepers.)

All this, I say, is innocuous and colorful, and animates the human scene. If this be the way youth wants to emphasize its singularity—singularity en masse, that is—and draw a line between its superior vision and that of the conforming, obtuse, working elders, who is harmed?

The deliberate cultivation of filth is another story. The glorification of dirt is a clinical signal of psychological disturbance. I feel sorry for the hippies who cannot know the psychological price they pay for this infantile regressing to the anal level. The "corruption and chaos" they reject, in their search for Arcadian innocence, is—alas—transported within themselves. Their hell is inside them. It is folly for adults to glamorize the hippies' weird cult. It is cruel to idealize mental illness as a new "youth culture."[35]

You praise me for

"speaking out for those students who are not news-worthy because they don't riot"

and add:

"Defend our wonderful Establishment!"

Well, the only "Establishment" I defend is the one called Reason. The most important aspect of our political Establishment is that it must respond to human needs, social inequities, economic dislocations. No other kind of structuring of power is as likely to give men a better life.

I do not think that temper tantrums are arguments—yours or those of the ones you hate. Adolescent terrorists may blare their idealism, but they shatter that consensus of civility that is the very core of a civilization.

Your omnibus defense and blind veneration of the *status quo* will not help us solve problems that must be solved—by intelligence, investigation, debate, criticism, votes, the final prevailing power of free men's free opinions.

"What do these spoiled students have to be so unhappy about in our colleges?"

They don't have to be spoiled to have a great deal to be unhappy about—*starting* with Vietnam and Cambodia, the tragic plight of many blacks, the polluted atmosphere, the rhetoric of Spiro Agnew, the filth in our waters, the demoralization of their teachers, the "soft, spineless mush [as one rebel put it] of the frightened Establishment."

If I were a college student, I would be made unhappy too: by gargantuan classes and bursting dormitories; by professors who hate teaching because it interferes with either their research or their ego expansion in off-campus committees; by an unexamined tradition that rewards those who publish trivia more than those who love teaching; by academic tenure, which scandalously pampers and encourages pedants to become fossils and lecturers to goof off; by academic practices that serve to subsidize scholars' hobbies and idiosyncrasies. The blithe indifference to students I have myself seen—among administrators, professors, tutors—is disgraceful.

I am not saying that solicitude will satisfy all grievances; students flock to huge universities *from* smaller colleges—then complain about the vast impersonality. Serious students say they would rather hear a first-rate scholar in person, albeit in a class of a thousand, than receive his regurgitated message from a fourth-rate instructor in a cozy class of twenty.

Walter Laqueur recently wrote:

> There is nothing more appalling than the sight of enormous aggregations of students religiously writing down pearls of wisdom that can be found more succinctly and profoundly put in dozens of books. There is nothing more pathetic than to behold the proliferation of social-science non-subjects in which the body of solid knowledge proffered stands usually in inverse ratio to the scientific pretensions upheld.[86]

If you think that Laqueur or I exaggerate collegiate evils (I speak from experience in and with the faculties of five universities), listen to an American who is no defender of our college rebels:

[This generation] is justly resentful of being fed into the knowledge factory with no regard to their individualism, their aspirations or their dreams.

Young men and women go to college to find themselves as individuals. They see the names of distinguished scholars in the catalogue and sign up for courses in the belief that they will learn and grow and be stimulated by contact with these men. All too often they are herded into gigantic classes taught by teaching assistants hardly older than themselves.

The feeling comes that they're nameless, faceless numbers on an assembly line—green cap at one end, cap and gown and automated diploma at the other.

Students want someone to know they're there.

The author of these words (hold your hat) is Mr. Ronald Reagan, Governor of California.[37]

But this does *not* mean we should turn our colleges over to emotional militants whose most conspicuous talent is their capacity to oversimplify problems the complexity of which they do not begin to comprehend. Not a single coherent, cogent program, in education *or* politics, has emerged from the eight years of student rebellion that have made a shambles of higher education.

Rabble-rousers (Right *or* Left) may have high IQs—but they are still rabble-rousers, no matter what songs they sing, with whatever lumps in their throats, with whatever dreams in their eyes. There were no greater idealists, expounders of noble goals (in their own eyes) than the Nazi students who flaunted "rights" they proclaimed superior to the lawful processes of what they too dismissed as a "bankrupt" system, a "hypocritical, fake" democracy. And a shameful legion of professors, in Germany and Austria, cheered them on.

Many rebels seem to think they should prevail *because* they dissent. This is muddleheaded: Dissenters have no greater moral or political rights than non-dissenters. Complaint contains no carte blanche sanctity; if it did, hypochondriacs should be kings.

"What has basically bugged these hippies and troublemakers anyway?"

The need for new kicks, demoralizing inner turmoil, a hope to escape from deadening boredom, a rage against discipline, frustration about one's helplessness to alleviate the visible, televised miseries of the world—all these create explosive energies. Political activism becomes immensely attractive to the bored, the thwarted, the weak, the power-thirsty. Politics becomes a form of therapy, an entertainment, an excitement, *fun*.

But let us be careful about distinguishing hippies from pacifists, reformers from revolutionists, Bohemians from delinquents, malcontents from thrill seekers who act out their hatreds in symbolic ways—substituting society for home, "pigs" for fathers, sex for masturbation, politics for personal aspirations.

Some young rebels are utopians; some are socialists; some are reformers with a strong and praiseworthy conscience; some are doctrinaire revolutionists; some are dreamers; some are neurotics; and some are so disturbed, so immune to reason or empathy or conscience, that we can only classify them, with compassion, as sick. Who but a psychopath could say, as did a member of the Weatherman faction, that the horrifying murder of actress Sharon Tate and her defenseless guests was a wonderful, "groovy" token of revolutionary import?

The parents of many young rebels, beholden to "progressive" and enlightened child rearing, confused liberalism with indecisiveness. Under a vulgarized and oversimplified Freudianism, they did not teach their young what is, and what just is not, permissible conduct to others. Parents who felt guilty about discipline, or were upset by temper tantrums, appeased stubbornness and rewarded rage. The folly of overpermissiveness, and a passion to *understand* their children, led generous parents to capitulate to the impulse-ridden demands of insatiable children. These parents forgot that infants need, seek, and *want* boundaries placed on their freedom. Boundaries are certain, protective, and reassuring.

Parents who do not block the psychological imperialism of the young win, not the young's love, but their contempt —for being weak, vacillating, bribable. For parents who do not govern with quiet firmness are thought not to *care* enough to risk their offspring's hostility. "They didn't love me enough to stop me from doing what I should not have been allowed to do." *The New Yorker*, some years ago, published a memorable cartoon about a nursery school, all bedlam and "free expression," in which one bewildered child asks the teacher: "Must we do anything we feel like doing? Isn't there *something* we can do that's forbidden?"

"Modern" parents damage their young by their weakness as parents; they avoid confrontations in the home (where it is healthy they first take place) by deferring, weaseling, giving in, and shelling out in the peculiar excesses of frantic acquiescence. Worst of all: They do not give their children a clear model of responsible, adult conduct. They know not the priceless value of the fructifying "No!"

I cannot help thinking that many militant students are unconsciously searching for adults, for adults who act as adults—without apology or ambivalence or guilt; adults not bamboozled by youth's impulses and irrationality; adults who do not surrender to hysteria and threat; adults who respond with clear, kind, swift rebuffs to those challenges to order and authority that are, at bottom, a cunning testing by the young of the moral confidence and certainties of their elders.[38]

Professor David Riesman says we are witnessing the rebellion of the first generation in history "who were picked up whenever they cried."

A good deal of the mystique of the apolitical flower children lies in their invitation to idyllic freedom. The hippie life promises a kind, giving, sharing, loving communality in which everyone is free to express his true self, free, especially, to throw off the shackles of sexual prudery and hypocrisy, to repudiate puritanical prejudices against, say, "mind-freeing" drugs.

But these promises also attract many deflowered wanderers who are severely disturbed, profoundly lonely, and dangerously alienated. Many psychiatrists and psychoanalysts (Rollo May, Erik Erikson, Bruno Bettelheim, Lewis Yablonsky, etc.) have noted that the truly gentle, loving young are defenseless against the incursion of psychopaths who "have had so few love models that even when they act as if they love, they can be totally devoid of true compassion. That is why they can kill so matter-of-factly."[39]

To me, the low-keyed, soft-spoken hippies seem sad and yearning and half-alive. Why do they *need* such bizarre dress and hedonistic devices? To help them *feel*, I suppose; to make them feel *anything*. They drift into debauchery, thrill-producing stimuli, drugs, orgies—to fill their inner emptiness with emotion, their mental emptiness with fantasies or hallucinations.

Is it not true that compulsive, promiscuous sex and compulsive, group perversities are signs of illness, not joy? The emancipated are victims of tyrannical demands on the self, no less than on the world they fear and profess to despise. Who or what can cure them? Not words. Not reason. Not argument.

"Why not show the young how wonderful our educational system is?"

It is certainly remarkable in what it has done—the greatest, widest mass education in history—and in what it can yet achieve. It is nothing short of revolutionary that our college population has doubled from 1960 to 1970—and septupled since 1930, when less than a million Americans were on campuses. Some of this expansion, of course, follows the growth in our population—and in the sixteen- to twenty-five-year-old age group; but most of it is due to the growth in the percentage of the young who go on to college. Most meaningful is the fact that so vast a number of those who go to college today are the children of parents who did not.[40]

But I hold a gloomy view about schools that can produce students and teachers who are so appallingly ignorant about (1) how this society works; (2) what the economic bases of a democracy must be; (3) what the irreplaceable foundations of civil liberty must be; (4) how conflicts between minorities and majorities must be managed.

The most damning indictment of our colleges is not "How come these punks aren't grateful for a chance to get an education?" but is seen in the number of students and young teachers who have become so hypnotized by revolutionary slogans that they have not wondered what would happen if Ku Klux Klan students in, say, Mississippi captured deans, "liberated" buildings, terrorized opponents, demanded the right to appoint or approve faculty, burned and bombed—

and demanded amnesty. What would the campuses of the North say?

The immature have always been dazzled by visions of paradise; they are drawn to romantic (the "in" word now is "charismatic") types—the Garibaldis, the D'Annunzios, the Trotskys, Castro, the quixotic Ché.

Our college militants are so ill-educated that they mouth the obsolete clichés of anarchism, the revolutionary nostrums Lenin dubbed "infantile Leftism," grandiose demands that demonstrate a plain lack of sense plus a lamentable ignorance of history.

"Student power," for instance. Nothing is more certain to destroy our universities. I am not playing Cassandra; I give you the record: Wherever students have exercised power they have ruined the school system; the best teachers leave, and the best students follow them. Student power is a guarantor of mediocrity, of political timidity, of silence on the part of independent or non-political students and professors. Look at South and Central America. Student power, there called co-gobierno, has beyond a shadow of a doubt ruined higher education.

What depresses me most about "our wonderful educational system" is that your destiny and mine, and the future of the rebels and their children, depend on the votes to be cast about such things as welfare programs, federal expenditures, price or wage legislation, tax policy—in all of which zones most of our faculty and students are ignoramuses.

I do not think we can reform or improve our schools as swiftly as the young desire; but we certainly dare not remain as rigid and traditionalist as your letters suggest. Changes *are* overdue—but changes for reasons we understand, to introduce measures we have reason to think sensible, to try to achieve purposes we agree upon as educationally and socially desirable.

Like most of our fickle race, students, teachers, preachers

take the achieved for granted; they forget *how much worse things can be made*. The road to Utopia, like the road to hell, should be paved with more than lofty intentions.

"Why doesn't anyone brand these troublemakers as the Communists they are?!"

Because there is no evidence that this is true.

That seasoned, full-time organizers are planning and fomenting protests, going from campus to campus, is becoming clearer each day. Of the six hundred students who immobilized a police car for many hours in Berkeley in 1964, over half, it turned out, had participated in previous demonstrations—and 15 per cent had been active in seven or more planned disruptions of the peace![41] The president of Southern Illinois University, testifying before the Illinois legislature, revealed that some of the leaders of the disturbances on the Champaign-Urbana campus were thirty years old, either non-students or part-time students expert in inciting violence. "We have no way to cleanse ourselves of them."[42]

And at Columbia, of 68 persons arrested on May 23, 1968, 46 turned out to be outsiders not in any way connected with the university. Of 705 persons arrested in "the big bust," 181 (26 per cent) were not connected with Columbia. And when the blacks caucused in Hamilton Hall, which they had seized, only half were Columbia students: the rest came from CORE, SNCC, and Charles Kenyatta's "Mau Mau" sect.[43]

It is immensely revealing that Leftist militants in American universities come from families that are, on the whole, more well-to-do than are those of either non-militant or

Rightist students. A study of the delegates to SDS and conservative YAF (Young Americans for Freedom) conventions revealed that Left-wing students come from families more affluent than Right-wing students, of whom the majority are the children of professional men, businessmen— and workers. Whereas the SDS has an insignificant number of proletarian offspring, the conservative and Right-wing ranks contain from one-fifth to one-third (!) students from working-class homes.[44]

Revolutionary eruptions, and the strategy of violence, do not mean Communist control or incitement. As a matter of fact, the Communists around the world sneer at "hooligan" youths; and the SDS thinks the Communist Party is an integral part of the system that needs demolition. True, Maoist and Castroist groups create student uproar, but they are splinter minorities who feed on the larger grievances— and the Communists are the first to curse these "Maoist *provocateurs*."

Some of the chants about Ho Chi Minh, Ché Guevara and Mao are not so much evidence of communism as of carnival, a rite that has its unwitting gallows humor, for the chanting celebrants know nothing about their icons. The young have always enjoyed baiting their elders with shocking symbols. The Left simply ignores what Mao and Castro stand for: totalitarian rule, fanatical repression, total despotism over the mind.

Our troubles cannot be laid at the feet of Communists, even though they no doubt welcome the well-known "death throes of capitalism." Our young rebels are rebels without an ideology. Of course, they want the war in Vietnam to end, the slums to vanish, all blacks to win equality, affluence, and respect, all injustice to be abolished. But where is a consistent (even wrong) analysis of the social ills they oppose? The student movement has its complaints, objections, enragements, demonstrations—but not a shred of program.

(Not one piece of legislation, for instance, has been proposed by the New Left.)

An amorphous hatred of *all* organizations, of any discipline, of any systematic theory that may cramp immature fantasies of instant success, of salvation through sensual satisfaction—these seem to me to characterize the elevated anarchism and hedonism of the young.

They are neo-Castroists, I think, without knowing it, romantic crusaders not unlike the well-to-do young Narodniki of Czarist Russia who abjured their comforts to champion poor peasants—and also scorned liberalizing reform. The sum total of their ideas was an unfocused love of man, a fuzzy populism that proved unrealistic and ineffectual.

Those who defend our students' revolt (I am not talking about student dissent) and try to conjure a program out of it end in verbose mishmash.[45] The most penetrating analysis of this aspect of student unrest was made by Professor Edward Shils:

> The transience of initial issues testifies not to the forgetfulness of the student radicals but to the fact that, however passionate they might be at the moment, they are not serious about the objects of their protest. But they are serious about something. They are serious about authority.
>
> . . . most of the student radicals are neither revolutionaries nor anarchists in the sense of meaning business. What they want to do is to annoy and frustrate authority, to bewilder it and enrage it. They wish to taunt it and cause it to lose control over itself and thus show their own ascendancy over it. They wish to humiliate authority and degrade it.[46]

What depresses me are the number of students, *not* Communists, who employ Communist/Fascist tactics: "confrontations" designed to force the campuses to call in the police —and then force the police to use force, which is decried and televised and shrewdly exploited.

Do our rebels ever reflect on what Mao has done to the

Chinese student cadres he encouraged? Or on what happens to students who criticize the Establishment in Moscow or Havana? Or that a mob is a mob, whatever its illusions? Or that Hitler's youth were intensely idealistic too, and vilified *das System*, the Weimar Republic, and reaped a whirlwind of insanity and war in which they too were destroyed.

"A Marxist like Professor Marcuse should not be allowed to teach at San Diego!"

Why not? What law has he broken?

Dr. Marcuse has a right to say or write whatever he wants—however woolly, silly, unsupported by data, or insupportable in logic it is.

But his competence and integrity as a teacher (and his innocence of technical economics) are for his colleagues—not you or me—to decide. If San Diego has no professors on its faculty able to punch holes in gaseous balloons, it should hurry to hire some.

Marcuse's murky ruminations can pass for profundity only among those hoodwinked by opacity of content and the torture of syntax. Dr. Marcuse, a *manqué* Marxist, was booed in Berlin by his own disciples, who now want to tear the city apart.

I doubt that many students actually read Marcuse, I mean read more than a token number of miasmic pages. His tired "dialectic" is a perverse hall of mirrors where free means slave, truth is false, real is illusory, classes are homogeneous, and superhuman masterminds of finance heartlessly exploit the groaning masses with affluence, while hypocritical lords of the press numb the public mind with the opiates of uncensored reporting.

Dr. Marcuse believes automobiles are a cunning device by which capitalist society channels off the revolutionary energy of the proletariat. He has also proclaimed that television diabolically saps viewers of discontent with their empty, materialistic, well-fed, newly furnished life. All this, according to the learned Hegelian, sanctions his preference for a dictatorship, a benevolent despotism—by approved evangelists, of course.[47] Dr. Marcuse's crowning work, *One-Dimensional Man,* is an excellent example of the best that can be expected from a one-dimensional mind.

Walter Laqueur, a seasoned student of student movements in Europe today and in the past, has concluded:

> The American youth movement, with its immense idealistic potential, has gone badly, perhaps irrevocably, off the rails. For this, a great responsibility falls on the shoulders of the gurus who provided the ideological justification for the movement in its present phase—those intellectuals, their own bright dreams having faded, who now strain to recapture their ideological virginity.
>
> The doctors of the American youth movement are in fact part of its disease. They have helped to generate a great deal of passion, but aside from the most banal populism they have failed to produce a single new idea.[48]

Incidentally, Dr. Marcuse, like you, the writers of rightist letters, wants to deny free speech to "certain" people; you and he differ only about whom you want to help via the blessings of dictatorship.

The radical Left might ponder Professor Marcuse's: "I would not go so far as to work for the destruction of the established universities: [They] are still islands, oases of critical thought. . . ." And Black Powerites should know that at a symposium at Rutgers University, Dr. Marcuse said that Negroes are brainwashed by our society and presumably cast their votes in a hypnotized manner; he declared that the civil rights movement could achieve nothing because American Negroes choose "middle-class values." And when Professor Sidney Hook "asked which situation he preferred—one in which the Negroes were *deprived* of their civil rights, including the power to vote, or one in which they freely exercised their civil rights to choose 'middle-class values,' [Marcuse] replied: 'Well, since I have already gone out on a limb, I may as well go all the way: I would prefer that they did not have the right to choose wrongly.' "[49] Such casuistry fills concentration camps.

✹   ✹   ✹

Finally, to my angry old *and* young compatriots: If we cannot in our colleges conduct debate without fist fights and catcalls and obscenities that drown out a speaker's words, if we cannot there pursue knowledge without partisan passions, where on earth can we?

> Men are qualified for civil liberty in exact proportion to their disposition to put moral chains upon their own appetites; in proportion as their love to justice is above their rapacity; in proportion as their soundness and sobriety of understanding is above their vanity and presumption; in proportion as they are more disposed to listen to the counsels of the wise and good in preference to the flattery of knaves.
>
> Society cannot exist unless a controlling power upon will and appetite be placed somewhere; and the less of it there is within, the more of it there must be without. It is ordained in the eternal constitution of things that men of intemperate minds cannot be free. Their passions forge their fetters.[50]

—LEO ROSTEN

P.S.   Once, after long and sober research, I estimated that 23 per cent of the human race are nuts. I was wrong. I am now convinced that 32 per cent are.

4. Who Speaks for the Young?

"Don't blame God—He's only human."
                              —The Author

Who speaks for our young?

According to every poll or study I have seen or heard of, the vast majority of college students, or those under thirty, do not support their self-selected spokesmen.

Militants make the headlines; they dominate our television; they paralyze schools; they terrorize teachers; they make martyrs. But whenever an all-inclusive poll is taken, the bellicose leaders are consistently rejected by those they say they are speaking for. The apostles of "truly representative, participatory democracy" turn out to be neither representative, participatory, nor democratic. They also have not read *The Federalist*, which saw the perils of a "participatory" system.

It is especially important to note how sharp is the division within the ranks of youth: between the activist minority of students (who choose generalized, liberal arts courses) and those in college who are working toward a vocation or profession. The gap between the orators and their generation is, of course, much greater when you compare those who go to college with those who go to work. Working youth seems overwhelmingly opposed to its "liberators."[51]

Item: Samuel Lubell's painstaking surveys of college youth on thirty-six campuses, for the Opinion Reporting Workshop of the Graduate School of Journalism at Columbia, revealed that only "around 10 per cent" of those interviewed showed any significant disagreement with their parents. Only one out of ten students "showed drastic changes from their parents." Over three fourths said they would vote for the same party as their parents. Lubell concluded:

"We found much less authority, and much less rebellion, than is popularly imagined."[52]

Item: The Adelson-Douvan study of three thousand twelve-to-eighteen-year-olds, from every economic and social stratum and all parts of the country, found few indications of serious conflict between American adolescents and their families. "On the contrary . . . it was more usual for their relationships to be amiable."[53]

Item: A *Fortune* poll revealed that over 80 per cent (!) of the young are "traditionalist" in their values.[54]

Item: A Louis Harris poll shows that 60 per cent of those in their twenties and teens oppose premarital sex, and 68 per cent want marijuana legally banned.[55]

Item: Vern Bengtson's study of five hundred students in three colleges in Southern California showed that 79–81 per cent of the students reported close, respectful, friendly relations with their parents.[56]

Item: The University of Michigan Survey Research Center's analysis of the 1968 elections disclosed that the proportion of voters under thirty who voted for George Wallace (in and out of the South) far exceeded the proportion among over thirties. (God spare us the extremists—Right *or* Left.)[57]

Item: A poll of students on seventeen campuses (in Illinois, Ohio, Michigan, Indiana, Kentucky) voted 75.2 per cent that "a person's disagreement with a particular law does not justify his disobedience to it."[58]

Item: As of July 1969, of the nation's 2374 colleges, violence erupted on 211; and one fifth of the student eruptions took place on six campuses.[59]

Item: The Guardian, a New Left journal, in 1969 estimated that the number of SDS activists ranged between 70 to 100,000—out of a college population of 7,000,000.[60]

I have no doubt that all of the above has changed since President Nixon's unbelievably lame, ill-timed announcement that he was sending American troops into Cambodia; and especially since the ghastly killing of four unarmed—indeed, apolitical—students at Kent State. (What possible justification was there for permitting young, inexperienced, trigger-jittery National Guardsmen to load their rifles with live bullets and permit—or order—them to shoot?) But the data offer an important lesson.

On the larger issue of "the generation gap," the hard evidence is even more surprising: Every study of which I, at least, know reveals that if you choose a statistically representative sample, the so-called generation gap is very small.

Professor Joseph Adelson, psychologist from the University of Michigan, has put the point most sharply:

> Is there a generation gap? Yes, no, maybe. Quite clearly, the answer depends upon the specific issue we are talking about. But if we are talking about a fundamental lack of articulation between the generations, then the answer is—decisively—no.
>
> From one perspective, the notion of a generation gap is a form of pop sociology, one of those appealing and facile ideas which sweep through a self-conscious culture from time to time. The quickness with which the idea has taken hold in the popular culture—in advertising, television game shows and semi-serious pot-boilers—should be sufficient to warn us that its appeal lies in its superficiality. From another perspective, we might say that the generation gap is an illusion, somewhat like flying saucers. Note: not a delusion, an illusion.
>
> There is something there, but we err in our interpretation of what it is. There is something going on among the young, but we have misunderstood it.[61]

The error lies, I think, in making dramatic generalizations from selected parts of the whole; in characterizing an entire generation according to its most vocal, flamboyant, or exhibitionistic platoons. Youths who hold jobs, and the college population that does not demonstrate, are neither dramatic, visible, newsworthy—nor threatening. There is no news in those who attend to their tasks and are dedicated to their studies.

Here is a letter that recently appeared in the New York *Times*—one of thousands around the land, no doubt, that pass unnoticed in a time when quiet voices are drowned out by bullhorns, when crowd-pleasers exploit primitive emotions, when mobs and marches command the attention of the mass media, when the convictions of the non-militant (and the pressures upon them) go unnoticed.

A hard core of defiant students [at Hunter College] are riding roughshod over . . . their fellow students and faculty members, with the malicious glee of those who know in advance that they will not be held accountable for whatever vile and vituperative utterances they choose to speak or print.

Student fees, a compulsory feature of all city colleges at present, are being used to pay for the printing of one student publication after another [that compete] in spewing forth scandalous slurs and obscenities, garnished with filthy illustrations.

Meanwhile, students who wish to attend classes have to toil up the stairs of the sixteen-story building to meet teachers who have done likewise, because [the militants] have seized the elevators. . . .

At a recent rally a young man, presumably a student, chided those of his fellow-students who complained. . . . His sarcastic advice was, "If you want to get to class that much, there's a stairway there, you know."

At the latest rally, held to "clarify the issues" to students, a young lady informed the faculty with drawling insolence that if they remained intransigent to present student demands for 50-50 representation on all faculty committees, including . . . Personnel and Budget, the students might just go ahead and "up our demands"—after all, "there are nineteen thousand students and one thousand faculty, and the Supreme Court has ruled: one man, one vote—that is democracy." Wild cheers and applause.

A FACULTY MEMBER[62]

Some of the recent writings of the young deserve response from some of us who were young and radical, too, passionately positive that this world was (as it still is) "untidy, unreasonable, and unjust." (The phrase is from London's *Economist*.) Let me quote from articles, conversations, and letters to me—from or about American youth today.

"The cynicism of your generation divided fathers and sons."[63]

What nonsense this familiar allegation turns out to be: *Some* sons simply *say* that fathers are "cynical." But their fathers may not be so much cynical as sensible—or experienced or stupid or unsure or chastened by reality or wearied by their efforts to "communicate" with the dogmatic and impassioned young.

The fathers I know can't be as cocksure about anything as adolescents are about everything. What is tearing *some* parents and children apart is not the cynicism of the parents but the arrogant, boundless, savage cynicism of their children.

We may blame fathers for their irresolution, their misguided propitiation, their fear of losing Missy's or Junior's love. But to all the fearful questions of our tormented age, honest fathers can give only troubled, halting answers. This is more useful and more honorable than giving slick, superficial ones—which may turn out to be catastrophic.

All of us—parents no less than children—are being battered by daily revelations of men's recurrent bestiality (whatever their color); by the horrors of Vietnam—and Cambodia; by the intractability of many of our problems; by the baffling parameters of poverty; by the discovery among American whites of the frightful price American blacks have paid for living in this land.

Yet our domestic problems *are* being ameliorated, and at a rate unprecedented in all history, or in any other country in this harassed world.

Our political temperature is made explosive by the intemperate and the bombastic, who have neither the discipline, the knowledge, nor the judgment to understand, much less solve, problems of confounding magnitude. The young may be excused for their ignorance; the adults who pander to them are unforgivable.

"Cynicism"? You make my hackles rise. Where, please, is cynicism more virulent than among the young who mock the efforts, diabolize the motives, and ignore the heartbreak of their elders?

"We'll have no leaders who enjoy handing out medals to war widows."[64]

Did John F. Kennedy enjoy handing out medals to widows? Did Roosevelt, Eisenhower, Jefferson? Abraham Lincoln's letter to Mrs. Bixby, who lost five sons in battle, would affect a heart of stone; whether it can penetrate heads of stone, I do not know.

Mao, Ché Guevara, Ho Chi Minh—whose ends and means I detest—also handed out medals to mothers and fathers and widows; but I would be ashamed to sneer that they enjoyed it.

"Material prosperity does not bring happiness!"

Quite true. It only helps make unhappiness more comfortable.

Our affluence has clearly not brought happiness to many (one may call them economic misdeterminists) who took it for granted that money would. And the discontents of the young are often the legacy of parents (liberal or once radical) who passed on to their children their own bitterness over ideals not realized, their disillusionment with gods who "betrayed" them (Stalin, Henry Wallace, Eugene McCarthy), above all, of adults who are acting out their guilt over having sold out their dreams or compromised their principles. Alas: The dreams were hopelessly utopian, the laudable goals were foredoomed because they rested on illusory economics, the political crusades showed a fatal blindness to the boundaries of the possible.

Panacea peddlers are forever being shocked by what they should know: the natural responses of ordinary men; the refusal of enough idealized People to echo and applaud self-anointed leaders; the failure of reality to change according to the desires or hopes or emotional needs of presumptuous saviors.

As for America's disappointing affluence: I, for one, doubt that money actually *hampers* happiness (except among masochists, a flourishing group). But money has clearly not suffused its possessors with that sublime peace of mind, that preening affirmation of virtue, that superior sense of altruism for which they hunger. So psychological compensation is found, among the well-heeled and guilty, in ardent, self-debasing money-raising for those who despise and promise to destroy them; and in fervent outcries of "Innocent!" "Persecution!" "Frame-up!" "Mistrial!"—before a trial is held, or any evidence disclosed, or any chance given for guilt *or* innocence to be tested. This is unjust to the innocent and undeserved by the guilty.

Men can be soured by success, as they are embittered by failure. For man really does not live by bread alone. (That is a quotation. It is from the Bible, an "irrelevant" old book that might be scanned before you reach thirty.)

As for happiness, the best society is surely the one that gives each man, woman, and child the best possible chance for health, education, security—by offering each of us the widest, freest ways of seeking, finding, or creating our particular kind of personal satisfaction without denying it, or the peaceful pursuit of it, to others. Our nation has not reached equal freedom, equality of opportunity, a communion of decency, the dominion of shared respect. But the efforts we make to achieve just that constitute the best reason I know for preserving the peace and the process of democracy. What our extremists, and their faculty allies, do not begin to understand is that the perfect can be the assassin of the good.

"Reason has betrayed us! Intellect is not enough!"[65]

Reason "betrays" only those who do not reason well or do not know what reason is.

Of *course* intellect is not enough. But who says intelligence excludes compassion, insight, a dedication to justice and change? Change, not chaos. Justice, not anarchy. Compassion is ill-served by attacking those who prefer reason to irrationality.

And if we reject reason, how can we know whether and why we really disagree? How can we appraise what is proposed, test its validity, clarify its consequences, judge its relevance (oh, yes!)? And what can you substitute for reason? Passion? Instincts? Dogma? Prejudgment? Ignorant sincerity, which encourages any hoodlum to mock knowledge and glorify his "gut" reactions?

Anyone with qualms about reason's role would profit from the analysis, and the careful consideration of reason's alternatives, in Morris Raphael Cohen's *Reason and Nature*.[66] The conclusions have yet to be faulted.

Hear Kingman Brewster, no apologist for the Establishment:

> Neither table pounding nor dreamy euphoria can be permitted to substitute for plausible argument. If impatience is not to be allowed to short-circuit argument with unsupported assertions, reason must be honored above the crude and noisy enthusiasms and antipathies.[67]

Göring said, "We [Nazis] think with our blood." Think twice.

Your fulminations against the reason that has "betrayed" you might be checked long enough to consider Voltaire's reply to Rousseau, who had written an essay exalting man's natural and noble instincts: "Your arguments against reasoning are so persuasive that one is almost tempted to get down on all fours."

"We will call off the debate on the phantom political issues that divided us in the past."[68]

Anyone who talks of "phantom" political issues knows nothing about American history. Or politics. Or economics. Or the democratic process.

You can't "call off" a debate, in a free society, just because you don't like the problems—or the answers.

"Our children will not be bound by the constraints of the mind that bind us. They will know instinctively what freedom is."[69]

To write that children will know "instinctively" what freedom is, is sweet, unmitigated delusion. It flies in the face of all we have learned about psychology, children, and the developmental process in man. Freedom is possible only when instincts *are* "constrained."

"Instinctively"? Dear God! Men are really not born trailing clouds of innocence. Instinctively, children are greedy, aggressive, selfish, impulsive, insatiable, egocentric, patricidal, matricidal, siblingcidal, and incapable of doing what can only be learned. Any nursery school can dismay, and edify, the starry-eyed.

I do not say that that is *all* that children are. Man's capacity for learning, for sharing, for controlling his instinctual drives, for loving and giving and deferring the gratification of his multitudinous desires has kept the human race from destroying itself.

As for "constraints of the mind"—they are certainly not unique to our system. Restraints make human societies possible; they are the cement of civilization. Men *must* moderate their infantile and instinctual demands. Freedom for Jack is possible only when Jill's instincts *are* "constrained." Vice is also versa.

Let me quote Bertrand Russell again:

> What people will do in given circumstances depends enormously upon their habits; and good habits are not acquired without discipline.
>
> . . . a person must learn while still young that he is not the center of the universe, and that his wishes are often not the most important factor in a situation. I think that the encouragement of originality without technical skill . . . is a mistake.
>
> Those who have rebelled against an unwise discipline have often gone too far in forgetting that some discipline is necessary.[70]

"We must free ourselves of the stereotypes, the greed, the anxieties and vapid status-symbols of our society."[71]

But what modern society, anywhere, does not contain stereotypes, greed, anxiety, status symbols? Social organization is a pyramid of power, status, respect—and resentment.

And where are stereotypes more conspicuous than among the young? And where are status symbols more puissant? A mare's-nest of vapid ideas characterizes youth's spokesmen. They preach pacifism with suspicious vehemence. They denounce injustice with unjust attributions of indiscriminate, group guilt. They parade their idealism with the most callous indifference to those they vilify.

"We will no longer waste our time debating . . . whether we should have a useless anti-missile system to protect us from imaginary enemies."[72]

I think it anything but a waste of time for Americans to debate issues of such awful magnitude. What is the alternative to debate? Decisions—by whom? In secret? Without criticism?

And how, *without* debate, can the lad who wrote that sentence possibly learn whether an anti-missile system is or is not "useless"?

Some scientists do not think the ABM complex entirely useless. The ones I know disagree about its comparative utility, and after umpteen hours of listening to, and reading about, the ABM, I am sorry to confess that I just don't *know* enough to call the ABM "useless."

As for "imaginary enemies": I shudder to think how many millions of innocent, peaceful human beings were starved, tortured, castrated, disemboweled, burned, slaughtered, starved—from 1939–45—because kindly soothsayers assured us the Nazi threat was just propaganda, and imaginary. (Read Leonard Mosley's remarkable *On Borrowed Time*. It will chill your blood. It should.)

I call it most dangerous to assume, and sheer madness to assert, that our enemies are "imaginary." Khrushchev said communism would "bury" us—and threatened war if Hungary was helped, or Suez taken. Mao has said he can absorb

300,000,000 (!) casualties. Red China, which just sent a satellite into orbit, will have thirty-five to forty-five intercontinental missiles by 1975.[73] They will be aimed *somewhere*—not "imaginary." The Russian ABM system, erected at stupendous cost, is almost completed. (Are they, too, so deluded as to erect a "useless" system?) And the ABM systems of others become powerful instruments of pressure and threat in the continuing *Realpolitik* of power among sovereign nations.

I deplore archaic sovereignties as much as the most dedicated advocates of world government do; but national sovereignties do, in fact, exist, and they fortify their power to defend—and deter. Whether anything can deter Red China, in time, is yet to be known.

Who would be fool enough to gamble our lives and our children's lives on unsupported daydreams about "imaginary" enemies and "imaginary" dangers? Besides, enemies become more real as the defenses against them appear to be ineffective. Weakness invites, and sometimes guarantees, aggression. Ask any Austrian, Pole, Hungarian, Congolese. What happened to Tibet? Korea? Czechoslovakia?

"It is one thing to smash powerless children on the picket line. It is a new game when the children begin assuming control of the country."[74]

But why assume that all God's children agree with you?

And when today's children do assume control, will they still be children?

Why, oh why, do you assume that your peers will never

change, or learn? I think they will. I respect their intelligence, their future response to future experience, more than you do—and certainly more than the advocates of idiot nihilism.

And note, please, the less than admirable ploy: "children." What kind of "children" are these who make bombs and burn buildings? The SDS, planning "four days of rage" in Chicago in 1969, obtained a permit for a parade, received resolute protection from the police (observers of the parade might have turned hostile), then broke away for senseless smashing of windows and roughing up of bystanders—for what purpose? The symbolic, the delinquent—and the publicity. What kind of "children" use clubs, chains, bricks?

Shall we pretend that all the vandalism and arson have not happened, and are not happening now? Shall we excuse crimes by employing that mask, "children"?

Children, my foot. At the Center for Advanced Studies in Palo Alto, rampaging students burned the lifelong research papers of a distinguished scholar from India. The offices of professors at San Francisco State College have been brutally vandalized. A young historian at Columbia lost years of work on a book, the manuscript of which was burned by the new, liberating knights of Attila. Teachers have been mauled, their tires slashed; they have fled their homes after threats of death.

Jerry Rubin, published by capitalist publishers, advises youth to dynamite the toll booths "because they charge money for people to get across free land." (Mr. Rubin seems to think that bridges and tunnels and highways sprout from the soil.) He also dreams of blowing up "Howard Johnson's on the turnpike—the universal oppressor of everybody."[75]

Funnier men have led lynch mobs.

"If everyone gave or received a daily, loving half-hour massage, wars would be over."[76]

The Romans *adored* massages, and were exceptional warriors and conquerors. I even hear that such massage lovers as Nero and Caligula were fond of strolling from their massage parlors to the arenas where, greatly relaxed, they fed unmassaged Christians to unmassaged lions.

In fact, the massaging may have increased the number of victims needed to satisfy the soporificated Caesars. To correlate muscle tone with peace is nuts.

"What we want is POWER TO THE PEOPLE!!!"

Which people? The American people have certainly not asked you to be their advocates, guardians, or governors. Nor do they approve or excuse your destructiveness.

Whenever movements that demand "ALL power to the people" have won power, the leader soon imprisoned, exiled, or executed those who resisted, or even questioned, a total concentration of power in one man's hands. If you think your generation or leaders will avoid this, you are certain to be disillusioned.

Whenever I hear that shining slogan, "Power to the People," I think of what happened in every single country where messianic saviors of the people took power. Russell long ago foresaw the inevitable:

By transferring economic power to an oligarchic State, they produced an engine of tyranny more dreadful, more vast, and at the same time more minute than any that had existed in previous history. I do not think this was the intention of those who made the Revolution, but it was the effect of their actions. Their actions had this effect because they failed to realize the need for liberty and the inevitable evils of despotic power.

Those who have been dazzled by the outward success of the Soviet Union have forgotten all that was painfully learned during the days of absolute monarchy, and have gone back to what was worst in the Middle Ages under the curious delusion that they were in the vanguard of progress.[77]

"Planned obsolescents can no longer run the country."[78]

But immaturity and inexperience will throw an intricate economy into chaos. Not one country ruled by ideologues or visionaries offers the slightest comfort to any who value their food and their freedom. Consider the record, on any continent, in whatever circumstances.

When a rebel has a toothache he goes to a dentist, not a demagogue. The rebels show less sense about politics, which is incomparably more complex than cavities.

In his dying days, it dawned on Lenin (who, Gandhi said, "took a terrible vengeance on mankind") that he had opened a Pandora's box from which came horrors he could not control.[79] Mao Tse-tung pours contempt on his colleagues for not having "stood up" to correct him before the fiasco of the Great Leap Forward. Why a member of any Central Executive Committee should "correct" its master—whether Mao or Stalin or Gomulka or Castro or Tito—who disposed of anyone, however faithful, who dared demur about his policy, is lost in the meretricious mysticism of "proletarian self-criticism."

"Pot is a lot less harmful than whisky. What hypocrisy it is for you who guzzle booze to punish us who smoke 'grass'!"

Pot is illegal; whisky is not.

I want pot legalized—to take it out of the hands of the pushers; then marijuana's content and distribution can be supervised.

But what makes you so sure that pot is harmless? How would you answer Dr. James Godard, former head of the Food and Drug Administration; Dr. Dana Farnsworth, chief of Harvard's mental hygiene program; the chairman of the AMA's Committee on Drugs; plus numerous other experts who agree that we just *do not know* what pot's long-term effects will be?

"At present we do not even have an accurate method to measure the potency of marijuana or hashish," writes one of the world's authorities on drugs and their psychological/ therapeutic effects: Dr. Nathan Kline, director of research at Rockland State Hospital, New York.[80]

It took thirty years to demonstrate the effects, on some, of cigarettes.

Besides, many young marijuana users now reveal that pot led them to far worse, nearly fatal drugs. And today's pot often contains deadlier stuff, because pushers want to make addicts.

In such a setting, it is surely the minimum of sense to say: Beware.

"We use four-letter obscenities to rub in the hypocrisy of your generation about sex!"

I give you Dr. Rollo May:

. . . it is dissimulation to deny the biological side of copulation. But it is also dissimulation to use the term f—— for the sexual experience when what we seek is a relationship of personal intimacy which is more than a release of sexual tension, a personal intimacy which will be remembered.

The former is dissimulation in the service of inhibition; the latter is dissimulation in . . . a defense of the self against the anxiety of intimate relationship. As the former was the particular problem of Freud's day, the latter is the particular problem of ours.[81]

"We will build a new freedom in love by our emancipation from the bourgeois taboos of the past."

Is today's sexual revolution more radical, or as wide in scale, as the one that took place in the 1920s and '30s? *That* sexual emancipation did not bestow mirific happiness on all who participated in it.

The determination of hippies to be autistic (which is not the same as being happy), to confuse discomfort with emancipation, to think obscenities a form of ethical progress, to confuse defiance with liberation, to sanctify mystical gurus and drug-induced hallucinations—these may be signs of sickness, not superiority.

The new sexual freedom has placed an awful burden on those who are physiologically unready for it, or psychologically unsure, or simply too young to make so grave a commitment.

> To the clinician, these casual relationships seem to be more miserable than not—compulsive, driven, shallow, often entered into . . . to ward off depression or emotional isolation. The middle-class inhibitions persist, and the attempt at sexual freedom seems a desperate maneuver to overcome them. We have a long way to go before the sexually free are sexually free.[82]

"We sleep around; you adults commit adultery. So what's the difference?"

Age. Emotional capacity. Judgment. Risk.

Among the *young*, sex without love extracts a special price. Therapists are telling us with increasing frequency that a sense of emptiness, and tormenting doubts about masculinity (or femininity), often possess those who find sexual partners too easily available or, as the hippies proclaim, "indiscriminate."

Those who court visions and "trips" through drugs, those who fornicate without commitment, those who spurn the "outmoded rituals" of love (and making love) are doing something perilous to their psyches. They are separating imagination from fulfillment. They are divorcing sex from love. They are mistaking physiology for emotion. Physical gratification without the enfolding aura of affection, courtship, respect, and shared pleasure takes a dreadful, however deferred, toll.

I say nothing about the frightful increase in venereal disease, illegitimate births, abortions, abandoned mothers. What tragedies attend this harsh new freedom!

". . . if you think we are so wrong then how do you explain why so many intellectuals, writers, and faculty members agree with us?!"

Given enough people, a surprising number will be found who believe that sunspots cause baldness, that Beelzebub is hiding in New Orleans, or that sense can be made out of the rantings of an Abbie Hoffman.

I am not impressed by the fact that instructors of English, eurythmics, sociology, or music become captivated by the appeals of the young, or in the name of Utopia NOW! Some professors, frustrated, romantic, long neglected, will rally to any cause, especially one that wins the approbation of the young and alleviates the boredom of their life (and their teaching), the spiritual barrenness of their material comfort, their guilt over being paid and protected to cultivate their gardens.

Professors can be as brainwashed as any true believers. They can embrace travesties of thought in politics they would laugh out of their laboratories. Surely it was a boo-boo of reasoning for a Harvard Nobel Prize winner to defend the students' pillage of a building, roughing up of adults, rifling of private offices, and printing of personal correspondence—by comparing it with the leaking of information in Washington! To compare a tip at the Press Club, or a *voluntary* disclosure or transmittal of a document—to compare these with mob action, burglary, and the shameless invasion of privacy was a form of ratiocination that stupefied many of the professor's colleagues.

I find more sensible and more admirable the position of teachers such as David L. Gutman of Michigan:

> . . . a large part of the intellectual life of the community has been put in the trust of professors; and we are not particularly faithful to that trust—when, out of fear or apathy, we give in to demands we do not in conscience agree with—whether they come from the regents or from protesting undergraduates.[83]

I remember the unbelievable spectacle of intellectuals who passionately defended the infamous Moscow trials, or the Stalin-Hitler alliance. Today, they idealize the New Left.

Not long ago, a distinguished American novelist (perhaps drunk, perhaps on pot) applauded random acts of political bravado—excusing, in effect, some hoodlums who had beaten up the owner of a candy store.

> . . . the chorus of bourgeois highbrows like [Norman] Mailer, [Kenneth] Tynan, [Dwight] MacDonald . . . and countless others . . . flatter the student radicals and assure them of how right they are in whatever they demand. Many members of this flatterers' chorus are middle-aged adults who seek the ardours of their youth in the vicarious exhilaration of "sit-ins" and strikes. Old memories of revolutions dreamed of in cafés and salons are revived, embittered disillusions of the Moscow trials and of the Hungarian Revolution of 1956 are dissipated by the thought of the new revolutionaries in the universities.[84]

But forget all I have said and consider your logic: Is it not foolish to support or defend an idea because of who champions it? The validity of a proposal has nothing to do with the rhapsodies of its proponents, the sex life of its opponents, or the propaganda its puppets employ to whoop it up.

"This system sponsors violence: Therefore, violence is needed and justified to overthrow it!"

Not as long as the system has legal, flexible, peaceful methods by which it can be changed—as, in fact, the United States *has* been changed, in the long, bloodless revolution since 1932. Why denigrate the power of protest?

Did not public protest force Lyndon Johnson to stop the bombing of North Vietnam? (Where, by the way, are those peacemaking responses by Hanoi—in Paris or on the battle-fields—we were assured would swiftly follow?) Has not public pressure forced American troop withdrawals in Vietnam? Did not radical rancors defeat Hubert Humphrey?

Violence is *not* justified in a democracy (as William O. Douglas argued in a Supreme Court opinion that preceded his most recent and more diffuse publication). And those who gleefully quote Jefferson's celebrated rumination about rebellion always fail to note that in another context he said: "It is the first duty of every citizen to obey the laws."

Once you open the door to admit violence—because the violent have a legitimate grievance, or had an unhappy childhood, or because it is Society that makes students miserable, or drives bomb throwers to kill—you offer immunity and encouragement to any crackpot, anarchist, or paranoiac to deal out death, at random. To pamper hysterics is to intensify turmoil.

"After what happened at Chicago in 1968, the pigs have to go!!"

I hold no brief for savagery—by the police or those who throw rocks or Molotov cocktails at them. Nor do I want the police to be replaced by political bully boys (yours or your opponents').

I repeat Churchill's maxim: "I cannot be impartial as between the fire brigade and the fire."

Mr. Tom Wicker of the New York *Times* wrote a moving personal threnody about the Chicago demonstrations, in which he wrestled with his responses to cry: "But these are our children!" True. And every Nazi had a mother. So do those—students, bystanders, policemen, firemen—who are always hurt in riots.

And if "the pigs" go, who will protect you from the wrath of the extremist Right—who are as violent and "dedicated" as you?

The Communists in Prussia voted for Hitler, against Hindenburg, in 1932 in order to increase and centralize "the repressive machinery of government"—which, they were deluded enough to think, they could then more easily capture. The defection of police power in Austria and Germany left the Left—and liberals, pacifists, intellectuals—with no protectors against the Storm Troopers.

What whirlwinds will you, bravely and blindly, reap?

"Capitalists deaden the minds of the masses through escapist movies and TV shows. . . ."

If not for television, would you or the American public ever have known how horrid and insupportable the war in Vietnam is? (Where are the television cameras to record the atrocities of the Viet Cong?)

Capitalists would swiftly lose their capital if they kept producing a product the masses did not like, want, choose, or support. The media are less prejudiced than the militants.

How intellectuals are offended by what the masses freely choose! Why shouldn't they watch TV? Or go to movies they like? The people can change the content of movies by the simple expedient of suspending their patronage, or the content of TV by the simple maneuver of turning their wrists. Viewing is voting. So is reading instead of viewing.

But why should television and films cater to intellectuals? And why watch that which you profess to despise?

As for "escapist," that bugaboo of puritans, it is psychologically invaluable, as Aristotle explained: the form of entertainment most people need and enjoy. "Entertainment" includes fiction, poetry, music, ballet. Each is an "escape."

Escapism is most prized in those countries where an all-wise, all-knowing cabal controls what the millions may see, hear, read, or say. Ask any tourist—or refugee.

"They [many parents] know reckless leaders are on the loose in America. They know . . . the present course is only leading to an eternal human blackout. . . ."[85]

But why believe such reckless ("they *know*") statements?

We all fear and dread the future, hence pay fantastic sums for deterrents. Who has a safer scheme?

As for prophecies of Armageddon, like the alarums and promises we once heard about what would happen if we were only *friendly* to Stalin, or the catastrophic effects of strontium 90, or what would follow "if we just stopped bombing North Vietnam"—an "eternal human blackout" is certainly not certain.

Even political Cassandras have modified their predictions. And Dr. Spock, an elder and parent and grandparent, now warns us of excessive permissiveness vis-à-vis our children, saying that he has been grossly misunderstood. He has.

"Man can no longer allow color television to suck his intellect down to the lowest common denominator!"[86]

What about black and white TV?

Once more the blinding cliché. Some TV is superb. Most is as banal as its viewers.

Was man's "intellect" really higher *before* TV? Do you

really think that before television existed, people spent their leisure hours discussing Plato, Mozart, Gresham's law? Or do you, as I suspect, want to impose *your* preferences on the audience?

How odd that those who profess to speak for the people so despise the people's tastes and choices. Again and again, in the United States, England, Italy, Japan, Poland, Czechoslovakia, etc., etc., television viewers switch from Shakespeare to soccer, from Ibsen to Westerns, from discussion programs to soap operas.

Snobs might pause to examine their assumptions. Why accord greater respect to a Ph.D. counting adverbs than to the man who can fix the Ph.D.'s furnace? Or repair his shoes? Or build his garage? Is it not hypocrisy to pose as lovers of the people—and despise them for their taste and their choices?

You may retort that your generation wants to elevate the masses and their culture. You can, of course, try—and learn from the experience. It is the publishers, the mass media, who constantly publicize, and print the propaganda of, the student movement and your articulate leaders. Would your dispensation do as much?

As for the young man I quoted verbatim ("Man can no longer allow color television to suck his intellect down to the lowest common denominator"): Exactly how is intellect "sucked down"? And do you mean the lowest common denominator or the largest common denominator? The lowest can't be the largest.

Now consider one item: Five million pre-school children who watched TV's *Sesame Street* made gains two and a half times as great as children who did not—in understanding numbers, letters, geometric forms, etc. And the children came from poor homes. And the gains were made after only six weeks.

Incidentally, *who* will no longer "allow" TV to show its programs? What a word for a libertarian to use!

Censors of the world, unite.

"We of the young generation still have not come to understand ourselves. We have been too nervous, too anxious, too guilt-ridden to really know what we are all about."[87]

And knowing that you don't know what you are about, O brave young knights, why not try to learn? Scorn is no substitute for insight.

Therapists tell us that an intransigent social conscience is often a disguise for personal, inchoate rage. Militants, like other mortals, try to deny their secret sense of unworth by the psychological mechanism called projection. This is best illustrated by the wife at a cocktail party who chided her husband: "Don't you think you ought to stop drinking, dear? Your face is already beginning to look fuzzy."

Dr. Bruno Bettelheim, to whom some student leaders came for therapy, concluded that the "exceedingly bright" leaders are surprisingly immature, "emotionally fixated at the age of the temper tantrum."[88]

And to those in the ranks of youth who do not understand themselves, as I and my generation did not understand ourselves in equally pain-ridden years, I suggest a slow reading of this observation by Konrad Lorenz:

> During and shortly after puberty, human beings have a tendency to loosen their allegiance to the traditional rites and social norms of their culture, casting doubt on their value, and look around for new and perhaps more worthy ideals. . . . If at that

crucial time of life, old ideals prove fallacious . . . and new ones fail to appear, the result is complete aimlessness, the utter boredom which characterizes the young delinquent.

If, on the other hand, the clever demagogue, well versed in the dangerous art of producing supra-normal stimulus situations, gets hold of young people at the susceptible age, he finds it easy to guide their object-fixation in a direction subservient to his political aims.

At the postpuberal age some human beings seem to be driven by an overpowering urge to espouse a cause, and—failing to find a worthy one—may become fixated on astonishingly inferior substitutes.[89]

I find it tragic to see students rampage like mindless buffaloes. I find it heart-rending to see "mind-freeing" (sense-dulling) drugs induce a premature senility. I think obscenity childish, neither art nor honesty. (What the young call hypocrisy is often only kindness or decorum.) I find it mind-boggling to see the young herds lock-step as their prophets cry "Liberation!" but mean "Confirm our caprices and our idiosyncrasies."

Perhaps when our present rebels become parents they will learn how frustrating temper tantrums are; what price we pay for overindulgence; how baffling adolescent defiance is; and how cleverly destructiveness, deployed by the emotionally tormented, can pose as idealism.

Self-doubt and self-hatred are often the source of that blind rage that is directed against the nearest, most vulnerable scapegoats: parents, teachers, the System or the Establishment. Within student organizations, yesterday's idols are today's liars or traitors.

. . . one finds little but cold hatred, in the minds of the student leaders, for the university and its purposes. They were not interested, really, in revolutionising the university. Their interest—a projection of adolescent romantic fantasy—was in revolutionising a social order and, with this, in destroying the university utterly.[90]

To those of you, the young, who still can listen, I say: Not *every* sickness is the fault of parents or teachers or society. Misery (among young or old) not only loves company; it reduces itself by fury against those it can blame. Some of the sources of your discontent surely lie within *you*—and your awareness of youth's inevitable inadequacy.

It takes time and effort and exertion to, say, learn calculus. It takes time and experience and self-discipline to become adult.

One crucial difference between children and adults is that children cling to their fantasies of omnipotence; adults have had to learn how to relinquish or revise them. Children want everything *"Now!"* (a revealing word in the slogans of the frenzied). Adults have had to learn how to wait.

Reason is not precipitate, nor common sense obsessive; and wisdom is surely not oversimplifying, or slave to unbridled impulse.

Themistocles' words, if you will look in Plutarch, may haunt you as they haunt me:

> Wife, the Athenians rule the Greeks, and I rule the Athenians, and thou me, and our son thee. Let him then use sparingly the authority which makes him, foolish as he is, the most powerful person in Greece.

5. Sermon

"To think freely is beautiful; to think justly is even more beautiful."

—THORILD

(Inscription over entrance to main lecture hall, Uppsala University, Sweden)

Dearly Beloved:

In his commencement address at Northwestern, Professor Bergen Evans began with a striking suggestion to the graduating legion:

> . . . when you can, steal a furtive glance behind you. You will see some of the most remarkable people ever to inhabit the earth—your parents and grandparents, the two generations immediately preceding your own.
>
> For these are the people who, within five or six decades, have increased life expectancy by approximately fifty percent; who have eradicated plagues; who cut the working day by a third [and] doubled real wages. These are the people who, building thousands of high schools and colleges, have made higher education—once a privilege of the few—available to many millions.
>
> These are the people who, without bloodshed, effected, in 1930, a social revolution which in its humane consequences makes the French Revolution seem a mere outburst of savagery and the Russian Revolution a political retrogression.
>
> These are the people who established the United Nations, who defeated Hitler, contained Stalin, and made Khrushchev back down.
>
> These are the people who, after spending billions in prosecuting a war, gave billions more, not only to their friends but even to their former enemies, so that the world would not plunge into a devastating depression.
>
> These are the people who soared outward into space . . . and downward into the atom, releasing for man's use . . . the primal energy of the cosmos.
>
> And while doing all this, they produced a great literature and an exciting architecture—indeed, stimulated extraordinary experimentation and creativity in all the arts.[91]

It is, of course, unavailing to expect the young to realize all that this means. It is small wonder that the early heralds of youth's passion, e.g., Paul Goodman, now find themselves disillusioned, chastened, and ignored by the flock whose cause they romantically championed.

One professor, who was quick to join one of the earliest campus crusades, recently said with some bitterness that it is absurd to expect the young to offer solutions to any of the problems about which they riot. It is a pity that the professor had to learn what a seventy-two-year-old Druse farmer recently said to an interviewer:

> If you give a child responsibility, he will ruin you. He is not prudent . . . he doesn't know what to do. He doesn't know how to spend the money and how to do his work. So I will not agree to give away any authority. I feel that I am wiser than my children; so I have to keep this responsibility.[92]

I am constantly surprised by the acrobatic fustian people accept as undisputed truth. It is asserted, *ad nauseum,* that a "growing percentage of our population is aged fourteen to twenty-five." This is very significant; it is also very wrong. The young are growing in numbers; but their *proportion* in the total population still stands around 20 per cent of the total. The median age in America in 1910 was twenty-four. Today it is twenty-seven years eight months. Population experts expect it to be around twenty-eight in 1985. We are getting older, not younger; there are more of us, and more who live longer, than ever before.

What *has* zoomed fantastically is the number of young who go to high school and college. Since 1950, high school enrollment has more than doubled; college enrollment has tripled.[93]

Over seven million (!) students in America today cramp our colleges: Seven million equals the combined populations of Rotterdam, Stockholm, Dublin, Belgrade, Liverpool, Oakland, Des Moines, Norway, and Iceland.

The magnitude of the repercussions of this number is only beginning to be comprehended. I, for one, do not believe there are seven million high school graduates in the United States who really want to go to college—to be educated. Their parents may push them to. And our affluence has made them economically obsolete: They have nothing else to do. (Virtuous Minimum Wage laws serve to bar many from working.)

If there are too many students in college, there also are too many too old to be treated as children. Our young mature physically at a younger age than their grandparents did (the onset of menstruation, for instance, has dropped six months each decade). We forget that the idea of the college acting as parent dates back to the time when college students *were* children: As late as the eighteenth century, college freshmen were thirteen and fourteen years old.[94] It is silly to subject a returned soldier, or a twenty-one-year-old girl devirgined in the eighth grade, to parietal regulations.

It is interesting that the students who complain most about too large classes, and being "robbed of identity," and being "mere numbers in an impersonal computer operation," nevertheless choose and continue to prefer the huge, overloaded colleges. Why? Because the large schools are more interesting, more challenging, more rewarding, and offer more choices. The smaller colleges, with one faculty member for each fifteen students, lose applicants (and honor students) to schools where the student population is greater than many townships. Branches of the University of California which are small, attractive, comforting, set in salubrious locations, have for years had difficulty attracting students, who continue to prefer the big caldron of Berkeley.[95]

I suspect we need five separate types of colleges now, for five distinct and not-to-be-mixed kinds of students:

1) Those who want to learn a vocation or trade.

2) Those attracted to the civilized ambiguities of a liberal, "useless" education.

3) Those who want to enter a profession.

4) Those who don't know what else to do with themselves for four years—and who are spared the necessity of earning a living by parents who want them to go to college because it's the right place to meet the best boys/girls.

5) Those who received so miserable an education in high school that they are certain to be humiliated and thwarted and made to feel stupid in college courses. They should certainly not be denied what every American deserves: a decent training in spelling, reading, geography, arithmetic, and an energetic education in American history and institutions. Call it college where high schools have failed.

I think we may all profit from the awareness that certain problems are not ours alone, nor the product of American family indulgences or deficiencies, nor—above all—the bitter fruits of a "heartless business civilization."

> Old men have assured me, in Mayan, in Navajo and in Arabic, that the young are lazy and self-indulgent, that they are given over to smoking, peyote-eating or drunkenness, that they do not uphold the important traditions, and that they are the spoilt children of affluence: "Life is easier now and so they do not want to work."[96]

Adolescence is an entirely new phenomenon in human society. (Puberty is another matter.) Adolescence is the product of modern, relatively affluent society—since, say, 1910. Before that, young men (and some young women) went to work around the age of fourteen. It would have been thought inconceivable that millions upon millions of the young would be prevented from doing anything useful, even during the long summer months when schools, for obsolete agricultural reasons, are closed.

The most neglected aspect of student revolt in America is the support it received from members of the faculty. They lent rebellion their names, their encouragement, their speeches—and gave them money for the furtherance of the cause. "Some eminent, powerful, internationally seasoned and immensely prestigious faculty . . . served the students well. Most of them [later] fled to other campuses or re- treated behind locked Institute doors, but in the beginning they served the student revolutionists well."[97]

In the balances of history, I think greater honor will be accorded teachers such as the young one who wrote this:

> Whether we like it or not, by becoming teachers we accept important power over the lives of students; accordingly, we have to be ready to show, when push becomes shove, that we have personal integrity to match that power.
>
> The generation gap in the universities begins in ourselves as teachers . . . in the gap between our own pretensions to intel- lectual leadership and our unwillingness to pay the price of the power that we seek.[98]

I wonder how those faculty members who aided campus revolt will come to terms with themselves in a calmer future. Did they not give away rights they would have refused to surrender to, say, an investigating committee of Congress, or a reactionary board of trustees, or a witch-hunting press? Did they not ask the law to close its eyes to actions they would never have defended had mobs come to the colleges from a construction site? Did they not provide excitable, immature students with the invaluable rationalization that violations of peace and law are moral, indeed admirable, once worthy slogans are mouthed? Did they not ask for am- nesty for acts committed on a campus which, if committed by their enemies—or in their neighborhood—they would have denounced with horror? Did they ask themselves what was the effect on the America beyond the college gates of making a campus a sanctuary for lawbreaking and an inviolable base, a "neutral" staging ground, for hit-and-run guerrilla raids off-campus? Did they not see what was plain to see: that the extremist Left is certain to provoke a frightening response from the extremist Right? Did they not understand that a revolution does not long shelter ecstasy or mass hysterias? Did they not see that persistent "confrontations" with the power structure are sooner or later bound to force police powers to be exercised? Were they really ready to accept Mao's dicta: "Power grows out of the barrel of a gun. . . . A revolution is not a tea party"? Did they think rioting a spectator sport? Had they no guilt about students who were beaten, teachers who were vilified, lecturers who were shouted down by neo-Nazi mob chantings? Had they no doubts when colleagues' offices were sacked, their manuscripts destroyed, their homes desecrated with painted obscenities, their families terrorized by telephoned threats of murder?[99] Did they shrug off as lamentable, "to be expected," or "sick" the making and planting of bombs by students who had been led to believe that extreme means are justified by noble ends?

What absurdity it is to call the university repressive or intolerant, a tool of sinister conspiracy, the enemy of progress and peace, the stifler of unorthodox ideas. It is academic freedom and academic tenure that allow the charges to thrive and proliferate until they verge on what can only be called paranoia. I know of no instructor, teacher, or professor who has complained that he could not teach or think or say or write what he believed. I know of no student who can truthfully say that he could not read or write or say anything he chose to.

The larger irony, which makes Right-wingers see red (in more ways than one), is that it is precisely the American colleges that have been the most prolific producers of free, unorthodox, radical ideas and leaders. The colleges were at the very center of the peace movement. The anti-Vietnam pressures began on our campuses and in national student and faculty sit-ins and teach-ins. The opposition to the draft was emphatically launched in our colleges. At Columbia, a poll of both the undergraduate and graduate faculties found that 70 per cent favored America's withdrawal from Vietnam when the rest of the population supported President Johnson.[100]

I wonder how decent men, whatever the accident of their color, can defend, say, the Special Co-ordinator of Black Studies at San Francisco State College, Mr. Nathan Hare, who, according to the local press, said in a public speech:

> They say we are too few to fight. We should vote. But I can kill twenty [white] men. I can cut one's throat, shoot another, drop a hand grenade in the middle of a whole bunch. I get only a single vote, and that's between the lesser of the two evils. . . . I don't believe in absolutes, so I do not categorically reject all white men—only 99 and 44/100th of them.[101]

How can serious men so confuse the issue of authority (not power) in a university? Students come to college because they lack knowledge. Can they possibly be competent to decide what they should learn, or how it should be taught, or by whom? The goal of those who teach is to go on teaching—that is, to stay in colleges; the goal of most students is to leave, the sooner the better.

How can one defend college quotas on an ethnic or racial basis? A quota that favors any group must, sooner or later, operate at the expense of another group. The most impressive academic performance by groups (to those who insist on thinking that way) is made by Chinese, Jewish, and Japanese students. Shall seven out of ten be asked, or forced, to leave? Or has "America known enough of anti-Semitism and anti-Oriental feeling to be wary of opening that box again."[102] Is not the problem to widen, not lower, the area of eligibility, without reference to color or creed, and without the introduction of criteria that are extraneous to education? How bitter is the paradox of liberals who, a decade ago, fought the practice of requiring college applicants to submit a photograph (which permitted discrimination against skin color or nose shapes or eye slantings) but today support the practice—because "How else can you identify the blacks?"[103]

My sense of astonishment is not limited to the campus. Consider the spectacle of the theorist of radical feminists, Ti-Grace Atkinson, addressing a conference of two hundred women, brought together by the State of New York's Women's Unit, of Governor Nelson Rockefeller's office and the National Conference of Christians and Jews. The liberating ladies applauded when Ti-Grace Atkinson urged them to "support the prostitute. . . . Go out on the street to help her. . . . The prostitute is the only honest woman left in America . . . because they charge for their services, rather than submitting to a marriage contract which forces them to work for life without pay."[104]

Nor does my sense of astonishment diminish when I read the editorials in dyed-in-the-blue organs of the Establishment. In the midst of a rash of bomb explosions and bomb scares, the New York *Times* editorialized: "Bombings must not be glossed over as the actions of idealistic if misguided revolutionaries; they are the criminal acts of potential murderers."[105] The potential murderers in New York included some students who had made Columbia a shambles, were martyred, by some members of the press, as pure victims of a brutal and repressive society, and were no doubt encouraged to extend their intransigent idealism to a monstrous conclusion. Another newspaper crisply noted:

> When members of the cultural elite feel a need to remind each other that bombers are not idealists, we can see that those who should be guarding the bonds have been tearing them down.[106]

I was mystified when friends who should have known better denounced the proposed building, by Columbia, of an $11,000,000 gymnasium, a proposal first made by the City of New York in 1959, which *59 per cent of the Harlem community had approved*. Mark Rudd and his guerrillas, who clearly had no interest in the gym but were hell-bent on committing *some* destructive act against Columbia, succeeded in stopping construction of the gymnasium. The muggings and thefts and terrorism on the site increased at a rate frightening to the residents, black or white, on Morningside Drive. It had been one of the purposes of the new gymnasium to reduce crime in the area through the daily presence and movement of students.[107]

> The worst effect of student violence has been to excite liberals who assume that behind every act of violence there is a condition of injustice, and who take it as their guilty responsibility to eradicate the cause.[108]

Those who encourage the militant young tell them that they are a new elite, the honest, uncorrupted ones who will abolish evil and injustice where previous men have failed. I cannot see why or how some special insight or superior wisdom proceeds automatically from being under twenty-five. Idealism *is* a common property of youth, but it is far from restricted to the young. Nor is idealism, in the young or the old, necessarily paired with judgment or knowledge or competence or plain sense. If patriotism, as Samuel Johnson said, is the refuge of scoundrels, then idealism is too often the refuge of ignorance.

I cannot help thinking that much of the student movement rests on the drive for immediate, continual, undeterred gratification of the senses. Anything that thwarts the whim of the moment is called "repressive." That this unbridled hedonism, at the expense of work, study, discipline, or knowledge, should be hailed as "liberating" strikes me as tragic. How rash to call this "the brightest, best-educated generation in history."

I cannot forget a psychiatrist's account of the famous congregation of young music lovers at Woodstock:

> And [I] heard the same stories that you got from the March on Washington—how wonderful that somebody shared his blanket with me; somebody shared his food with me; we had a wonderful time, we sat up all night, sang all night, drank all night. . . .
>
> Youth has a tremendous need to get together in large groups, to get intoxicated by the image of each other's presence. I cannot be too impressed by the external forms because I see the underlying need, which is the same—to escape loneliness, my isolation; to find a reaffirmation that I am a worthwhile person in the fact that so many other people do the same things I do.[109]

One of the principal victims of the storm that has swept our campuses is the sense of history, a continuing glance at the past and its meaning, a charting of where we were and where we moved and where we are and where we can or should be heading. History is not a barren chronicle of dates and names; it is the retracing of human problems, efforts, errors, successes by which we may have some context within which to think and judge, some light to guide our search for causes and effects, some signals of warning, some tested beacons with which to light our voyage toward a wider, deeper humaneness.

Even a passing knowledge of that Pandora's box in which are treasures called Justice, Freedom, Equality, Peace, Security—and poisons such as Poverty, Prejudice, Irrationality, Killing, Hate—even a surface knowledge, I say, must lower the mature man's expectations of the imminence of a millennium.

The agitated think money or legislation, fervor or evangelism can swiftly set things right. But the men who know most (I am not among them), the men who have studied with care what we presently do know about a given field or conflict or policy, will agree with Daniel Bell:

> That political liberalism is in crisis is quite true, but perhaps not for the reasons given by the student Left—in fact, for reasons that would not be to its liking. For if there is a single source for the crisis of liberalism—apart from the Vietnam War—it is the complexity of our social problems, the linked nature of change, and a lack of knowledge (or adequate research) about where and how one can effectively "cut into the system" in order to direct social change. The old simplifications about "more" schools and "more" housing, or even "better" schools or "better" housing, have not proved very useful in breaking the cycle of poverty or in dealing with Negro family structure. For those given to moralisms or "sophisticated" chatter about "power," such talk about complexities is irritating . . . they regard it as an evasion of the "real" problem.[110]

This is a bitter lesson to learn; and the young, as I and my friends in the Thirties, resent and resist and deny it. I can only urge today's crusaders for justice to reflect for a moment on the fact that not *all* of the unhappy are right. Not *every* grievance is justified. Not *every* inequity proves that a malevolent society caused it. And not every hammer means that something needs smashing.

Democracy *is* a slow, troublesome, frustrating, hazardous way of trying to solve persistent human problems. It shows us all its baffling ailments: injustice and insufficiency, corrupt men and debased methods, fitful disorders and fevers, and that impassioned disputation that frightens those who have not learned that the hottest arguments take place within the family.

> The [democratic] public is constantly reminded, in the most vivid way, of the evils in its own society and in those other countries where television is free to prowl. But the evils of life in closed totalitarian countries cannot be given anything like the same emphasis. All of which tends to lead to a grossly distorted view of the world.[111]

The rebellious young, whose dissent and protest deserve the highest respect (just as their virulence and violence do not), are part and parcel of that way of ordering our lives that makes it possible for us to grow, to invent, to improve —without censorship, blackmail, force, or fraud.

It was Whitehead, I think, who said:

> The art of free society consists, first, in the maintenance of the symbolic code; and secondly, in fearlessness of revision. . . . Those societies which cannot combine reverence to their symbols with freedom of revision, must ultimately decay. . . ."

Where, then, do I end? With a sense of sorrow that a polemical tract such as this is necessary in the seventh decade of the twentieth century. With the conviction that words do matter, and ideas do count, and debate is imperative. With a plea to those who use violence—whether in deeds or slogans—to consider the carnage and chaos they may bring down upon themselves, and us.

Senator Margaret Chase Smith recently made a prediction I would urge the young to read with care:

> Extremism . . . is increasingly forcing upon the American people the narrow choice between anarchy and repression. And make no mistake about it, if that narrow choice has to be made,

the American people, even if with reluctance and misgiving, will choose repression.

Ironically, the excesses of dissent in the extreme left can result in repression of dissent. For repression is preferable to anarchy and nihilism to most Americans.

It is time that the greater center of our people, those who reject the violence and unreasonableness of both the extreme right and extreme left, searched their consciences, mustered their moral and physical courage, shed their intimidated silence, and declared their consciences.[112]

How do I close? With the certainty that nothing is more sacred than the unflagging pursuit of truth, whomever it may disappoint or contradict or upset. With a renewed commitment to the surpassing miracle of a society in which men are free—even to extol folly, or mock experience, or pursue false gods, or say things that make me shiver. Consider this concluding passage from Edgar Z. Friedenberg's sprightly article "The Generation Gap":

If the confrontation between the generations does pose, as many portentous civic leaders and upper-case "Educators" fear, a lethal threat to the integrity of the American social system, that threat may perhaps be accepted with graceful irony. Is there, after all, so much to lose? The American social system has never been noted for its integrity. In fact, it would be rather like depriving the Swiss of their surfing.[113]

The frivolity of the simile makes me shudder. If the American social system "has never been noted for its integrity" it has certainly been noted for suffering and supporting professors who publish such sweeping, sociomorphic non-science.

Democracy, and only democracy, has structured power in such a way that social change can proceed legally, peacefully, without the horrors of purges, the insanities of fanaticism, the suffocating imposition of dogma. This tormented century has driven home more forcefully than ever the lesson that that nation will prove most enduring which is most resilient, most moderate, most just, most adjustable to the inevitable strains and pains that accompany social change. Freedom of criticism, freedom of argument, freedom for the unorthodox to challenge the prevailing consensus is still the first and final bastion free men must defend.

To such men, fear is a poor response to delirium. The English journal *The Spectator* recently remarked:

> The threat to the universities lies not from the students, but from the reactions of the authorities. By pandering to the student "leaders," by treating the game as if it were much more than a game, the university authorities run two risks. The first . . . is that they will encourage the popular backlash against public spending on university education. Few ordinary people, as it is, have much time for the spurious grievances of what they see as a pampered minority. The student leaders may succeed in "radicalising" their middle-class contemporaries; they are succeeding even better in "conservatising" the proletariat.
>
> But the second and far greater danger is that, because they lack the confidence to defend the institutions they are meant to lead, and the liberal values those institutions are meant to represent, they will by their own actions destroy the universities and everything they stand for. If a whiff of the Weimar republic lies over Britain today, it is not difficult to discern where the blame lies. Not with the students or self-styled enemies of the established order, but with the guardians, both in the universities and elsewhere, of the most precious institutions of our civilisation, who have lost the will and the self-confidence to fulfill their trust.[114]

The only force I fear more than human irrationality is irrationality armed with passion. It is endemic to our common, many-colored race. Perhaps these pages will help reduce unreason's malignant growth.

Reference Notes
(Guaranteed Relevant)

1. "Rhetorica," in *The Basic Works of Aristotle,* ed. by Richard McKeon (Random House, 1941), p. 1404.
2. A remark made by Frederick Mosteller, Professor of Statistics, Harvard.
3. See Chapter 4.
4. Daniel Bell, "Columbia and the New Left," *The Public Interest,* Fall issue, 1968, pp. 85, 87. See also the comprehensive analysis by Arnold Beichman, "Letter to Columbia," *Encounter* (London), May 1969, pp. 14–26.
5. Joseph Adelson, "What Generation Gap?", New York *Times Magazine,* January 18, 1970, p. 10 ff.
6. John Fischer, "Four Choices," in *Natural Enemies,* ed. by Alexander Klein (Lippincott, 1969), pp. 387–88.
7. "If Not Reason, What?", *American Scholar,* Spring 1970, p. 250.
8. Quoted in A. H. Raskin, "Berkeley Five Years Later," New York *Times Magazine,* January 11, 1970, pp. 28–29.
9. Ibid.
10. Robert A. Nisbet, "Who Killed the Student Rebellion?", *Encounter* (London), February 1970, pp. 10–11.
11. Bergen Evans, Commencement Address, Northwestern University, June 14, 1968 (privately printed).
12. See the statistics and tables in New York *Times Almanac,* 1970, p. 647 ff.
13. See the numerous daily dispatches, from Havana and Moscow, during March and April 1970 in the New York *Times,* Washington *Post,* etc.; or the accounts in *Newsweek, Time, The New Leader,* etc. from January through June 1970.
14. Yale Brozen, "Welfare Without the Welfare State," speech to Montpelier Society in Tokyo, September 9, 1966 (privately printed and distributed).
15. Irving Kristol, "What Business Is a University In?", New York *Times Magazine,* March 22, 1970, p. 111.
16. Carleton Beals, *Great Guerrilla Warriors* (Prentice-Hall, 1970), p. 219.
17. See the essays by Professors T. S. Ashton and W. H. Hutt in *Capitalism and the Historians,* ed. by F. A. Hayek (University of Chicago, 1954); Joseph Schumpeter, *Capi-*

talism, Socialism and Democracy. (Harper & Row, 1963); John Jewkes, *Public and Private Enterprise* (University of Chicago Press, 1965).

18. Bertrand Russell, *Portraits from Memory* (Simon & Schuster, 1969), pp. 8, 136.
19. *American Scholar,* Autumn 1969, pp. 606–17.
20. *The Guardian* (New York), June 26, 1969, quoted in Z. Brzezinski, *Between Two Ages* (Viking, 1970), p. 224, footnote.
21. Bernard Berelson and Gary A. Steiner, *Human Behavior: An Inventory* (Harcourt, Brace & World, 1964), section on prejudice.
22. Those who think there was no race prejudice prior to the white man's imperialism might profit from H. A. C. Cairns' remarkable *Prelude to Imperialism* (Routledge and Kegan Paul, London, 1965); or Stanislav Andrevski's *The African Predicament* (Atherton Press, 1968). For an illuminating study of Central and South American variations on the theme, see Andrevski's *Parasitism and Subversion* (Weidenfeld & Nicolson, London, 1966). The literature on prejudices in India, Pakistan, Indonesia, China, and Japan is too vast to mention, but K. R. Minogue's brilliant and brief *Nationalism* (Basic Books, 1967) is a good opener.
23. Native employers in Africa or India are harsher on their help than are white employers. And Greek, Portuguese, Yugoslav laborers in Germany and Switzerland say they are treated with greater fairness there than in their native lands. (See Andrevski, *The African Predicament,* p. 28 ff.) For further readings in race and prejudice: George E. Simpson and J. Milton Yinger, *Racial and Cultural Minorities: An Analysis of Prejudice and Discrimination* (Harper & Row, 1965); Edgar T. Thompson and Everett C. Hughes, eds. *Race: Individual and Collective Behavior* (Free Press, 1958); UNESCO: *Race and Science: The Race Question in Modern Science* (Columbia University Press, 1961).
24. Quoted in New York *Times,* April 30, 1970, editorial.
25. Daniel Bell, op. cit., p. 80.
26. *The Public Interest,* Summer issue, 1968.
27. *Measure for Measure,* Act I.
28. The U. S. Bureau of the Census figures in the New York *Times,* August 20, 1969. Also see *Economic Growth in the*

United States, Committee for Economic Development, October 1969, and *Capital Formation and Economic Growth*, National Bureau of Economic Research (Princeton, 1955). The most exact study of poverty, and the most rigorous definition of its indices, was made by Mollie Orshansky: "Counting the Poor: Another Look at the Poverty Profile," *Social Security Bulletin*, U. S. Dept. of Health, Education and Welfare, January 1965.

Also see "Why Are the Poor With Us?", *The Public Interest*, Fall 1965, pp. 71–95, articles by Professors Nathan Glazer and Eveline Burns.

29. *Report of the President's Commission on Income Maintenance* (U. S. Printing Office), November 12, 1969.

30. See, among others, E. J. Mishan, *21 Popular Economic Fallacies* (Allen Lane, London, 1969); Yale Brozen, "The Untruth of the Obvious," speech in Los Angeles, March 14, 1968; Joseph Schumpeter, op. cit.; Milton Friedman, *Capitalism and Freedom* (University of Chicago Press, 1962); *Capital Formation and Economic Growth*, National Bureau of Economic Research, op. cit.

31. *Economist* (London), May 10, 1969, p. 51.

The problem of poverty is not as simple as it may seem: it entails variations in cost of living, free services, etc. Income, by itself, is an unreliable index: It ignores the differences between, say, a retired lawyer widower, who owns a mortgage-free home and gets along on $3500 a year, and a laborer with a family and installments to pay on his home, car, and furniture, who fares badly on $5000 a year. (See *The Public Interest*, Fall 1965, from which the above data were condensed.) Only the rich had indoor toilets a century ago.

A study of poor Manhattan families (45 per cent Puerto Rican, 30 per cent Negro, 25 per cent white) with a median income of only $3300 per year, revealed that 95 per cent own at least one television set, almost 50 per cent own an automatic washing machine, and just about as many own automobiles as is true in Manhattan's middle class. The overwhelming majority (85 per cent) bought only new, not used, furniture; over 40 per cent paid over $300 each for their TV sets. See David Caplovitz, *The Poor Pay More* (Free Press, 1965), which analyzes data from the Bureau of Applied Social Research, Columbia University.

32. Mark Gerzon, *The Whole World Is Watching* (Viking, 1969), p. 26; and Robert S. Liebert, "Radical and Militant Youth: A Study of Columbia Undergraduates," presented before the Association for Psychoanalytic Medicine, April 1, 1961, p. 28 ff.

33. Alexander Gray, *The Socialist Tradition: Moses to Lenin* (Harper & Row, 1959), p. 189.

34. Obtainable from Government Printing Office (Washington), dated January 31, 1970.

35. For a valuable survey and dissection, see John R. Howard, "The Flowering of the Hippie Movement," *Annals of the American Academy of Political and Social Science* (Philadelphia), March 1969, pp. 43–56. Also see the comments in David Dempsey, "Dr. Bettelheim Is Dr. No," New York *Times Magazine*, January 11, 1970.

36. "Reflections on Youth Movements," *Commentary*, June 1969, pp. 39, 41.

37. Speech to Commonwealth Club, San Francisco, June 1969, quoted in A. H. Raskin, op. cit., p. 85.

38. See the remarks of Walter Laqueur, John R. Howard, Robert A. Nisbet, Bruno Bettelheim, *Encounter* (London), September 1969, pp. 29–42. Edgar Z. Friedenberg, "The Generation Gap, *Annals of the American Academy of Political and Social Science*, March 1969, pp. 32–42, holds strongly different views. See also Edward Shils, "Plenitude and Scarcity," *Encounter*, May 1969, pp. 37–57; and the illuminating remarks of Erik Erikson in "The Embattled University," *Daedalus* (Cambridge), Winter 1970.

39. Dr. Lewis Yablonsky, quoted in *Time*, December 12, 1969, p. 25.

40. *The Public Interest*, Spring 1970, pp. 133–34.

41. Seymour M. Lipset, "The Activists: A Profile," *The Public Interest*, Fall 1968, p. 48.

42. Delyte Morris, in Chicago *Tribune*, May 26, 1970, p. 2.

43. Daniel Bell, op. cit., pp. 71, 81, 84; also see Daniel Bell's "Quo Warranto?", *The Public Interest*, Spring 1970.

44. S. M. Lipset, op. cit., p. 46; Professor Lipset also quotes material from a study by Braungart and Westby.

45. See, e.g., A. Mendel, "Robots and Rebels," *New Republic*, January 11, 1969; or the more ambitious, Manichean musings of Theodore Roszak, *The Making of Counter-Culture* (Doubleday, 1969).

46. Edward Shils, op. cit., p. 37.
47. See "Marcuse Defines His New Left Line," New York *Times Magazine*, October 27, 1968, pp. 29–31 ff.
48. Walter Laqueur, *Commentary*, June 1969, p. 40.
49. See Sidney Hook, Letter to the Editor, New York *Times Magazine*, November 10, 1968, p. 22.
50. "A Letter from Mr. [Edmund] Burke to a Member of the French National Assembly" (1791), quoted in R. J. White (ed.), *The Conservative Tradition* (Nicholas Kaye, Ltd., London, 1950), pp. 57–58.
51. Joseph Adelson, "What Generation Gap?", New York *Times Magazine*, January 18, 1970, p. 10 ff. A provocative psychiatric analysis will be found in Bruno Bettelheim, "The Problem of Generations," *Daedalus*, Winter 1962, pp. 68–96.
52. Samuel Lubell, "That Generation Gap," *The Public Interest*, Spring 1969, p. 53.
53. Quoted in J. Adelson, op. cit.
54. Ibid.
55. Louis Harris, "Poll on Current American Values," *Life*, January 9, 1970, pp. 102–6.
56. J. Adelson, op. cit.
57. Ibid.
58. D. C. Beggs and H. Copeland, Chicago *Tribune*, January 15, 1970, section 1-A, p. 1.
59. Washington *Post*, July 2, 1969.
60. *The Guardian* (New York), January 11, 1969.
61. J. Adelson, op. cit., p. 36.
62. Letter to the Editor, New York *Times*, April 2, 1970, editorial page.
63. Roger Rapaport, "Why We Need a Generation Gap," *Look*, January 13, 1970, p. 14 (New York area issues only).
64. Ibid.
65. Paraphrased from William Hedgepeth, "A Vision of the Human Revolution," *Look*, January 13, 1970, p. 60.
66. Morris Raphael Cohen, *Reason and Nature: An Essay on the Scientific Method* (Free Press, 1953).
67. Kingman Brewster, "If Not Reason, What?", *American Scholar*, Spring 1970, pp. 250–51.
68. Roger Rapaport, op. cit.
69. Ibid.
70. B. Russell, op. cit., pp. 10–11.
71. R. Rapaport, op. cit.

72. Ibid.
73. *Atlas* magazine (New York), December 1967, p. 7.
74. R. Rapaport, op. cit.
75. Jerry Rubin, *Do It!* (Simon & Schuster, 1970), *passim*.
76. Bernard Gunther, a "sensory-awareness pioneer" quoted by George Leonard, "Why We Need a New Sexuality," *Look*, January 13, 1970, p. 54.
77. B. Russell, op. cit., pp. 136, 231. For a profound, exhaustive, and prescient analysis of the consequences of joining economic to political power, under whatever ideology or rubric, see Joseph Schumpeter, op. cit.
78. R. Rapaport, op. cit.
79. See Robert Payne, *Lenin* (Simon & Schuster, 1964); Bertram D. Wolfe, *Three Who Made a Revolution* (Dial, 1948); Adam B. Ulam, *The Bolsheviks* (Macmillan, 1965); Robert Conquest, *The Great Terror* (Macmillan, 1968); Harold Shukman, *Lenin and the Russian Revolution* (Putnam, 1966); Leonard Schapiro and Peter Reddaway, *Lenin: A Reappraisal* (Pall Mall, London, 1967).
80. Dr. Nathan Kline, "Psychiatry in Ferment," New York *Times*, Special Supplement: "Annual Education Review," January 12, 1970, p. 77.
81. Rollo May, *Love and Will* (Norton, 1970), p. 47.
82. J. Adelson, op. cit., p. 34.
83. David L. Gutman, New York *Times*, Special Supplement, January 12, 1970, op. cit.
84. Edward Shils, op. cit., p. 47.
85. R. Rapaport, op. cit.
86. Ibid.
87. Ibid.
88. Bruno Bettelheim, "Obsolete Youth," *Encounter* (London), September 1969, pp. 29–41.
89. Konrad Lorenz, *On Aggression.* (Harcourt, Brace & World, 1966), p. 258.
90. Robert A. Nisbet, "Who Killed the Student Rebellion?", op. cit., pp. 10–11.
91. Commencement address, June 14, 1969 (privately printed and distributed).
92. Reported by David L. Gutman, op. cit.
93. See the respective tables in the New York Times Almanac and the World Almanac.
94. Henry Steele Commager, "Students in Rebellion," *Natural*

Enemies?, ed. by Alexander Klein (Lippincott, 1969), p. 121.

95. See Seymour M. Lipset, Daniel Bell, op. cit., and articles in "The Embattled University," *Daedalus*, Winter 1970.

96. Reported by David L. Gutman, op. cit.

97. Robert A. Nisbet, op. cit., p. 14.

98. D. L. Gutman, op. cit.

99. See the remarks by Professor John Bunzel of San Francisco State College, in "Black Studies at San Francisco State College," *The Public Interest*, Fall 1968, p. 28 ff.; and the New York *Times*, *Daily News*, and New York *Post* reports on the University Coalition, May 22 and May 23, 1970. Also see the dramatic firsthand account of Robert Brustein, "When the Panther Came to Yale," New York *Times Magazine*, June 21, 1970, p. 7 ff.

100. D. Bell, op. cit., p. 88.

101. Quoted by John Bunzel, in the New York *Times*, May 23, 1970.

102. Daniel Patrick Moynihan, quoted ibid. For a most instructive exchange on the quota system, see the letters of Judge Macklin Fleming and Dean Louis Pollack of the Yale Law School, in *The Public Interest*, Spring 1970, pp. 44–52.

103. Bunzel, op. cit.

104. New York *Times*, May 29, 1970, p. 30.

105. New York *Times*, March 13, 1970, p. 38.

106. *Wall Street Journal*, March 23, 1970, p. 12.

107. D. Bell, op. cit., p. 64. Also see Roger Starr, an authority on housing, "The Case of the Columbia Gym," *The Public Interest*, Fall 1968.

108. William Letwin, "Democracy and the English University," *The Public Interest*, Fall 1969, p. 139.

109. Bruno Bettelheim, quoted in David Dempsey, "Dr. Bettelheim Is Dr. No," New York *Times Magazine*, January 11, 1970, p. 108.

110. D. Bell, op. cit.

111. Robin Day, "Troubled Reflections of a TV Journalist," *Encounter* (London), May 1970, p. 81.

112. New York *Times*, June 2, 1970, p. 1 ff.

113. "The Generation Gap," *Annals of the American Academy of Political and Social Science*, March 1969, p. 42.

114. *The Spectator* (London), March 7, 1970, p. 295.